How Just Is the Market Economy?

How Just Is the Market Economy?

Edward Dommen

WCC Publications, Geneva

Cover design and photo: Rob Lucas

ISBN 2-8254-1399-2

© 2003 WCC Publications
World Council of Churches
150 route de Ferney, P.O. Box 2100
1211 Geneva 2, Switzerland
Web site: http://www.wcc-coe.org

No. 104 in the Risk Book Series

Printed in Switzerland

Table of Contents

Preface

In our contemporary world, powerful market forces of the global economy daily exacerbate the crises of global injustice, environmental destruction and poverty. Increasingly, communities and individuals involved in economic activity are called upon to rise above the cold logic of the market and, instead, to demonstrate new models of genuinely creative coexistence informed by a robust ethical perspective and love. This conclusion epitomizes the message of *How Just Is the Market Economy?* Edward Dommen provides a clear critique of and alternatives to the neo-liberal market economy as he informs us of its ideological, theoretical and practical assumptions.

The question "How just is the market economy?" is a difficult one, but Dommen succeeds in bringing to the fore a number of controversial issues that require thoughtful reflection. His argument is that the market alone cannot attain the ultimate objective of prosperity for all people on earth while at the same time protecting our mother earth. Within the market we are confronted with speculation, exploitation, inequity and inequality, dynamics which cannot be resolved alone by tools at the disposal of economists. The right tools are in the domain of ethics and revolve around the essential teaching, "love one's neighbour". According to Dommen, rather than focusing on the failure of markets, attention should be paid to the failure of love.

Dommen applies the biblical standard for trade – justice and taking the side of the poor. He is critical of the current market system which is limited to advocating for fair payment, transparent relationships and respect for life, placing limits on the extent of exploitation, yet which can achieve little more than mere equality of opportunity for all individuals to compete without hindrance. The author reflects the finding of many in the contemporary ecumenical movement that such equality has served only to help the clever and the strong to get ahead. Dommen provides readers with a high-resolution profile of the market and of its shortcomings as a just distributor of resources, particularly to the poor. The author highlights biblical passages and the ethical teachings of early Christian theologians as aids to an economic critique, and he shows how these sources suggest alternatives to the current theory and practice of the market.

Loving one's neighbour as an ethical criterion, which Dommen draws from Christian ethics, runs parallel to similar principles found in Buddhism, rabbinic Judaism, Islam and other religions and philosophies of East and West, North and South. The book condemns the greed inherent in the world's market economy. For instance, why should the market continue to allow 20 percent of the world population to consume 83 percent of global resources, or why should 5 percent of the world population consume 25 percent of the world's oil? Such greed is not merely a matter of making excessive or even illicit profits. It is a matter of monopolizing resources far in excess of one's own needs in a world where the basic needs of many people are not met. An alternative to the ethic of greed is found in an extension of the principle based in love of neighbour. The principle of love can transform and redirect the energy of human desire towards revitalization and growth. We are challenged to see the resources of the world as linked to the needs of people.

Edward Dommen is a member of the Ecumenical Advocacy Alliance's trade strategy group and a member of the World Alliance of Reformed Churches' task force on "Covenanting for justice in the economy and the earth". Concerns about global trade raised in these circles resonate in Dommen's treatment. The ecumenical discussion of trade has underlined the need to distinguish between a growing economy that fosters just, sustainable and participatory communities and an economy that aggravates inequality, social disintegration and damage to the environment. The current structural inequalities in the global trading system lead to a form of economic growth that undermines rather than enables the development of viable communities in north and south.

A fundamental restructuring of trade institutions is required before trade can meaningfully aid development. A variety of consultations organized through ecumenical organizations, in Asia, Africa, the Pacific and Europe, has evidenced a growing inequality and environmental destruction due to trade liberalization. Dommen analyzes the neo-liberal approach that has fostered inequalities and joins in requesting that priority on the trade agenda be given to equity, ethics and human rights. This book is a helpful tool in creating a consciousness of the way injustice is embedded in the theory and practice of the market, and hence it is a valuable contribution to the ongoing campaign of the Ecumenical Advocacy Alliance, "Trade for People, Not People for Trade".

Dommen raises a number of technical issues and leaves them open to further reflection. He issues a clarion call to re-examine the market presuppositions concerning competition, cooperation, individualism, entitlements, settling market disputes, collective goods, just prices, profits, external costs and the environment. He confronts the pundits who defend a neo-classical market model. Unless this debate becomes part of the multilateral and bilateral trade negotiations of our time, the world will never become a home for sustainable and participatory communities that participate in nurturing our planet.

The author has provided readers with ample food for thought.

Rogate R. Mshana
Programme Executive for Economic Justice
World Council of Churches

Introduction

This book is about economic ethics. It has chosen to concentrate on one corner of the field: the market. It is a typical corner in that the problems found in it are the same as those found in other economic corners. It has the advantage of familiarity. Starting from questions with which we have all been confronted, we proceed to explore a wide range of issues. By discussing the market we can discover how ethics may be brought to bear on the workings of the economy as a whole.

The market covers a large part of the world economy and an even larger part of the economy in developed countries. Furthermore, there are powerful pressures to extend its coverage. Since the collapse of the centrally planned economy in Central and Eastern Europe, the market has become a triumphant ideology. But the market is not the only conceivable means of organizing an economy. Political processes, administrative regulation, convivial sharing, home production to meet one's own needs are other ways of determining how much of what should be produced for whom. Each one has its particular advantages and disadvantages.

There is an elegant theory of the market, elaborated by means of mathematics from a set of initial premises. However, as we shall see later, the assumptions on which this theory rests do not correspond to reality in essential respects. Taken strictly, the market cannot function as theory says it should. To give it the status of a dogma is therefore dangerously arrogant. Nonetheless, the market is a handy device which can do a number of useful things. It is rather like the bumble-bee: the laws of engineering can prove that the bumble-bee cannot fly, but since the bumble-bee has never studied engineering it goes ahead and flies anyway. The market should be used pragmatically whenever it works better than the other tools available.

In short, "market" is a name given to
- an ideology,
- a formal theory, and
- a practical device.

Each draws strength from the others, sometimes improperly. It is important always to be clear in our discussions about the level at which we are talking.

No dramatically simple conclusions will emerge from our explorations. The market, like so many subjects, is made up of a complex set of components which interact in intricate ways. Conclusions will therefore have to be modest, tentative and always open to revision.

However, it does seem incontrovertible that, while the market is a convenient way of solving a wide range of secondary economic problems, it cannot cope unassisted with the fundamental ones. If you want to choose a nice tie or swimsuit, the market is just the thing. If you want to be sure that essential needs are fairly and correctly met, you shouldn't count on the market: other mechanisms are better suited.

This book concentrates on the ethical features of the market economy. It begins with a brief description of what the market is (chapter 1); in chapter 2, it describes what the market can actually do before focusing more specifically in chapter 3 on aspects of it which raise ethical problems. Finally it confronts the way the market economy intersects with various concepts of justice (chapters 4 through 8).

Let us state at the outset the basic principle underlying the whole of the argument. The fundamental social imperative is that each of us should love our neighbour as we love ourselves (Matt. 22:39). This goes beyond the golden rule that one should treat others as one would like to be treated oneself (Matt. 7:12): it involves an obligation to give priority to the poor, the weak and the marginalized. Which passage can we single out to illustrate this insistent message of the Bible as a whole? Perhaps Matthew 25:31-46. In short, this broadside concentrates on justice between people as humanity's part in the alliance between God and humankind.

> I was hungry, and ye gave me food: I was thirsty, and ye gave me drink: I was a stranger, and ye took me in: naked, and ye clothed me: I was sick, and ye visited me: I was in prison, and ye came unto me. Then shall the righteous answer him, saying, "Lord, when saw we thee hungry, and fed thee? or thirsty, and gave thee drink? When saw we thee a stranger, and took thee in? or naked, and clothed thee? Or when saw we thee sick, or in prison, and came unto thee?" And the King shall answer and say

unto them, "Verily I say unto you, inasmuch as ye have done it unto one of the least of these my brethren, ye have done it unto me". (Matt. 25:35-40)

Abbreviations

CFC   chlorofluorocarbons
GATS   General Agreement on Trade in Services
IMF   International Monetary Fund
OECD   Organization for Economic Cooperation and Development
WCC   World Council of Churches
WTO   World Trade Organization

1. What the Market Is

Meanings of the word "market"

The word "market" has a wide variety of meanings. Some of the more common ones are presented below. It would be possible, but fastidious, to attempt a more exhaustive classification or present a more detailed one. That the word "market" is used in so many ways and has so many shades of meaning reflects the central place of markets, of trading, in our culture.

A place where buying and selling occur: This use of the word is now mainly historical in the developed countries. It is recalled in place names. In Britain there are towns called Newmarket, Wickham Market, Market Drayton, Market Weighton and so on. Zurich has a Marktgasse, a Marktplatz, a Neumarkt and a Rindermarkt. Today we find supermarkets and even hypermarkets dotted about our towns and the countryside.

For some, the market is not just a physical space, but a magical one. "The market is a magical space where prodigies occur. When goods change hands they remain identical; yet the exchange produces a 'plus' for the seller as for the buyer... That is the extraordinary event: everyone gains. In the eyes of orthodox economists the prestige which the market enjoys will never be dimmed."[1]

A potential outlet: This may be a geographical area: Swiss watches are selling well on the Far Eastern market; there is strong resistance to genetically modified food in the European market. The word may also refer to a particular social category: teenagers constitute a distinct market for clothes or leisure activities. The elderly are increasingly being solicited as an attractive market.

A set of transactions between buyers and sellers: In this sense, "market" may refer to occasions on which many goods may be traded: there is a weekly market in this neighbourhood or that town. The St Ours fair in Aosta, Italy, has been held annually on 30 and 31 January for over a thousand years.

"Market" may also refer to the set of transactions and operations concerning a particular good or service. One talks of the metals market or the labour market. In this sense, the market does not necessarily involve buyers and sellers meeting in one place. Transactions on the foreign exchange market for instance are largely carried out by telephone or electronically. One can hire a rental car – to be collected in a particular geographical location of course – by dealing with a call centre which could be located anywhere.

The state and evolution of supply and demand: One may say that the labour market is tight or that the copper market is falling. In this sense, the word "market" is shorthand for the relations between supply and demand at a particular moment.

The price system as a way of guiding behaviour: When one says "let the market do its job" or one talks of market mechanisms or market-based policies, one is talking of the price system as a way of guiding behaviour.

The market economy in its context

The market economy is an example of the use of the word in the latter sense of mechanisms that shape behaviour. In the market economy, supply and demand play a decisive role in determining what is to be produced, in what quantities and to whom it is to be allocated. The market is only one of several possible ways of organizing a society's economic relationships (Fig. 1).

Fig. 1: The place of the market in the economy

The economy:
production, distribution and consumption

The money economy

The market economy

Not counting …

A money economy is one in which exchange involves money as a medium. The market economy is undoubtedly its most elaborate form, but other expressions of it can be found.

Of course exchange between separate buyers and sellers is involved, in which money changes hands. However, it does not necessarily involve prices determined by supply and demand. The price may simply be an administrative notion in an institutional arrangement where the quantities exchanged are determined by other considerations; this was often the case in the centrally planned economies in Central and Eastern Europe before 1989. The price might in other cases simply be a convention to underline that the transaction falls outside other forms of relationship current in the society. Thus in rural New Hebrides (as they then were), where pawpaws grew in everyone's garden and only the odd traveller would need to buy one, the stated price remained at 2 shillings long after the currency was decimalized and the shilling abolished.

The economy involves the whole set of processes of production, distribution and consumption. It need not involve money. Exchange may also take the form of barter.

Indeed, the processes need not even involve exchange. Distribution may be organized by administrative allocation as in the centrally planned economies.

The economy may be organized by feudal or prebendal relationships:[2] production and its means belong to the chief of what in many cases may roughly be described as a clan. The chief distributes the goods produced among the clan's members or clients, or indeed beyond, according to the traditions, needs and interests of those concerned. In prebendal systems, both the act of giving the product of one's efforts to one's chief and the chief's act of redistributing it serve to build and maintain the community.

Whether the fruits of the economy are distributed by exchange or by other means, an essential purpose of economic relations lies in communication, in weaving the cloth of community:

> Charge them that are rich in this world, that they be not highminded, nor trust in uncertain riches, but in the living God, who giveth us richly all things to enjoy; that they do good, that they be rich in good works, ready to distribute, willing to communicate. (1 Tim. 6:17-18)

Calvin insists repeatedly on communication:

> If God had wished to keep everyone in isolation, then we would not have the necessity that compels us to mix with each other. Whatever people may wish, they must communicate with each other. So we have to come back to this: we have to know, in fact, that God wanted to make us members of one body.[3]

Notwithstanding what has just been said, production which is directly consumed within the household is also a form of economic activity. It involves neither exchange with outsiders nor, as a result, recourse to money. In the past it has accounted for the bulk of the economy in many rural societies. It continues to be important today in several parts of the world. It is the very life of many poor households. Indeed, the immense respect which it deserves is all too often denied it, if only because it is invisible to economists who can see only what is reflected in economic statistics composed exclusively of monetary magnitudes.[4]

Above all, it must be remembered that any kind of economy supplies only part of humankind's needs. God fed the people with manna "that he might make you know that humanity does not live by bread only, but by every word that proceeds from the mouth of the Lord" (Deut. 8:3).

Even within the domain of the economy, the starting point is the boundless generosity of God – "who giveth us richly all things to enjoy" (1 Tim. 6:17) – and all the things which proceed from it: the gift of creation, of life itself, of God's grace. And in our daily lives the greatest pleasures lie in beauty and conviviality, which stretch beyond the economy. The space outside the circles in figure 1, labelled "not counting..." is the most important part of the diagram, the foundation on which all the circles rest. The best things in life are free.

This book focuses strictly on the market, not on the economy in general and even less on those aspects of life which lie beyond it. In particular it eschews ethical problems which arise in any form of economy, in order to concentrate on those which arise specifically in the market. Furthermore, it examines only the limits of the market, the zones where ethical problems lie. It ignores the area – and it is a large one – in which the market serves humanity well.

Some features of the market economy

The market economy may be defined more or less strictly, that is, more or less dogmatically. Here we shall describe some of its characteristics in a manner broad and flexible enough to cover the range of situations found in real life.

Through the mechanism of *supply and demand* buyers and sellers by and large determine the price of goods and services. The prices thus determined guide production decisions, and thus the assortment of goods offered on the market. This mechanism ignores those who lack economic power.

In particular, it ignores those who are too poor to make their wishes felt in the market. The market may be likened to a voting system in which each unit of currency corresponds to one vote. Those who dispose of more units have more votes; the poor have few or none.

Similarly, it ignores *future generations*, since they are not present to make their wishes felt by buying and selling on the market. The ethical issues lurking in the needs of future generations have only recently come to the surface, as the impact of human activity on the environment has only just become so substantial as to have consequences which will inevitably be felt by several generations. It was given public prominence by the World Commission on Environment and Development in its report *Our Common Future*, which dates back only to 1987.[5] That report asserted the requirement to meet "the needs of the present without compromising the ability of future generations to meet their own needs".

Most transactions concern not only the buyer and the seller but also people who are involved willy-nilly. The market ignores these people, who are the object of *externalities*. They are discussed below.

The economy covers more than allocation, however. Its *size*, for instance whether it is big enough to provide work for everyone who wants it (full employment), or its *rate of growth* are also economic decisions. For some people these matters should also be left to the market, while for others they call for a different order of decision to be taken by a consciously political process. The term "market economy" is sometimes used to include the latter type of system and sometimes restricted to the type of economy in which issues like unemployment and economic growth are left to the free play of market forces.

Sometimes adjectives are added to specify a type of market economy to emphasize particular aspects of the spirit in which it is intended to function. "Social market economy" or "liberal market economy" are examples.

The above describes the standard model of the market economy. Some people insist on certain optional extras as well.

One of these options is a sufficient degree of *competition*. This finds expression in the anti-trust laws of economies like the United States or the European Community. Perfect competition exists when the market consists of such a large number of buyers and sellers that no single one of them can influence the price by his or her individual behaviour. One must beware of arguments which defend the market economy by assuming that it corresponds to a state of perfect competition, since cases in which no single agent can influence the price are exceedingly rare. Try and imagine one!

There are those who contest the existence of a market economy if property is owned by collectivities and in particular by the state. They maintain that the market economy requires the *private ownership* of property and in particular of enterprises (the ethical issues raised by property in a market context are explored in chapter 5).

There are also those who associate the market economy with little as opposed to extensive government regulation. The market ideology is used to defend the *deregulation* which has been such an important feature of the domestic economies of the United States and the United Kingdom since the last two decades of the 20th century, as well as an important ingredient of the IMF medicine for sick economies.

It is important to note that the word "regulation" has meaning only in so far as the regulator is specified. Every social system functions by definition under some kind of regulation; otherwise, it is not a system but disorder. It is important for an ethical examination of any social, including economic, system to ascertain who sets the rules, and consequently in whose interests.

Reflecting the market ideology, the rules of the World Trade Organization restrict the freedom of governments to regulate important areas of domestic as well as international policy; in that sense, it promotes deregulation. On the other hand, the WTO rules are constrictive in their own right: they impose their own form of regulation. Thus the WTO can claim to be at the same time both an instrument of deregulation and a force of regulation – indeed some of its defenders claim that it is the sole rampart between order and disorder in international trade. The claim is difficult to sustain in that some form of order has existed in international trade ever since it began, although it has of course not always been the same system.

The market as a theory

It can be established mathematically that, under certain theoretical conditions, perfect competition has a number of desirable consequences. The market can be described in terms of a mathematical model. If all the assumptions of the model hold, the market ensures that every good or service is produced to the point where the cost of producing an extra or marginal unit corresponds exactly to the price a buyer would just be willing to spend to acquire an extra unit (in the jargon of the model this willingness corresponds to the buyer's marginal utility). If these conditions hold for every good and service, then no one can be made better off except at the expense of making someone else worse off.

This condition, technically called a "Pareto optimum", is obviously not the best of all possible economies. For instance, it takes for granted the initial distribution of income between all participants, no matter how unequal it may be. By ruling out the option of making anyone better off at the expense of anyone else, it gives the impression of treating each participant equally. In fact it expresses an exacerbated individualism, pushing it to the point of refusing to compare the relative merits of one person's needs with another's. It thereby denies in particular the preferential option for the poor so rooted in the teachings of the Bible. (The actual phrase "the preferential option for the poor" comes from the social teaching of the Catholic church, its first official appearance being in the encyclical *Sollicitudo Rei Socialis* of 1987, para. 42; but the concept is of course far older and widely shared among Christian denominations.)

A theory, known as "the theory of the second best", establishes by strict logic that if just one of the conditions of the model of perfect competition does not hold, or more precisely if just one price is not equal to the marginal cost and marginal utility, there are no logical grounds in terms of the "Pareto optimum" for striving to ensure that the other prices meet that condition.

THE THEORY IS FALSIFIED

Some of the conditions required cannot, however, exist in the real world. For example, no human being has perfect knowledge of the future. Imagine that a firm has just invented a new chemical product. The product may or may not do serious damage to the environment, but it will take twenty years after the product has been in widespread use before one can be sure whether or not it does so. The firm wishes to put it on the market now. If the product does no damage to the environment, the price should correspond only to the cost of production, but if it does do damage, the price must be higher to take this element of cost into account as well. Which price should the firm set, given that it is impossible for it to know now which scenario will turn out to be true?

The example is not theoretical; it has actually occurred. Chlorofluorocarbons (CFCs), invented in the 1930s, found wide application after the second world war as aerosol-spray propellants, refrigerants, solvents and foam-blowing agents. They are colourless and odourless; they are not inflammable or corrosive. They are extremely stable, inert compounds that are entirely harmless to humans in direct contact. Ideally inoffensive! However, studies undertaken during the 1970s revealed that CFCs released into the atmosphere accumulate in the stratosphere, where they have a deleterious effect on the ozone layer. CFCs have in short been found to pose a serious environmental threat. The discovery was so important that the scientists concerned, Molina, Rowland and Crutzen, were jointly awarded the 1995 Nobel Prize for chemistry as a result.[6]

That example has at least two implications for this book. Firstly, the market cannot stand as a scientific theory: according to the theory of scientific method, one case is all that is needed to falsify a scientific theory.[7] Secondly, as a consequence of the first, any argument for trying to set a price at the point where marginal cost equals marginal utility – or at any other point for that matter – depends on the merits of the particular case, in the light of a wide range of considerations including ethical ones. It does not depend on the overall workings of some grand model purportedly drawn from science.

You can't fence the market like a playing field

The market is not a playing field fenced off from the rest of human activity. All aspects of human life shade insensibly into each other.

COLLECTIVE GOODS AND SERVICES

Among the goods and services which economies furnish there is a category called collective goods. These have the property that, if available to any one person, they are by the same token available to everyone. A street light is an example: if it lights the road for one passer-by, it lights it for all. Selfish consumers will naturally pretend to be uninterested in the service or at least will systematically understate the amount they are willing to pay for it, since they are confident that other users will accept to pay for it in their stead. (This widespread kind of behaviour incidentally says something about people's truthfulness and the depth of their spontaneous love for their neighbour. Christian social teaching has from its inception been battling these aspects of human nature.) In any event, a frequent response is to remove such goods from the market and finance them through compulsory payments – i.e. taxes – in order to ensure that everyone pays their fair share.

While it could be argued that collective goods simply mark a boundary to the area where the market functions, that would be an over-simplification. The production of collective goods and services uses inputs which are traded within the market economy. The collective goods contribute to the overall demand for them and thus influence their price. Market prices can be determined solely by the free and competitive interplay of supply and demand only in an imaginary world in which there are no collective goods.

> Because the [market economy] refuses to recognize... collective needs, its very logic causes the multiplication of problems of a collective nature (in the economic, social and ecological fields); but because of its fundamental individualism, the same logic simultaneously multiplies obstacles to the creation or functioning of institutions which could deal with these collective problems...[8]

Knowledge is a quintessentially collective good: if you teach someone something you know, you do not deprive yourself of the knowledge as if you had given someone an apple which you might otherwise have eaten yourself. One could even argue that by communicating your knowledge you actually improve it, since the effort of communication increases your mastery of the subject. The market economy tries perversely to transform this collective good into a private and exclusive one, preventing the free flow of knowledge by imposing artificial barriers to it in the form of intellectual property rights like copyrights and patents. To hinder in this way the free flow of knowledge and ideas indispensable to the health of an open society is to score an own goal on the playing field of the market economy.

THE MARKET INVOLVES MORE THAN BUYERS AND SELLERS

Only unusual and trivial transactions in the market economy exclusively involve a buyer and a seller. In most cases third parties are also involved willy-nilly. In more technical terms, economic transactions normally involve "externalities".

Externalities may take the form either of costs or benefits. An external benefit occurs when the transaction generates a pleasant consequence for someone who was not a willing party to it. If a housewife buys flowers to put on her balcony, that is a transaction between her and the florist. Yet all the passers-by in the street will share in the pleasure of their beauty, at no cost to themselves. If on the other hand a smoker buys a packet of cigarettes to smoke in a café, the act imposes damage on the health of the other customers: that is an external cost.

If externalities are to be taken into account within the market economy, external costs and benefits need to be internalized, in other words to be reflected in the prices facing the buyers and sellers so that they take their decisions in the light of the full range of the economic consequences of their act. Full internalization can however have perverse effects. The issue took a practical political form in the early days of the railway in the United Kingdom, in the early 19th century. Parliament passed a law to the effect that if sparks from the smoke stack of a locomotive set fire to a cornfield next to the line, the railway would not be responsible for the damage. The argument was that if the railway were liable to pay compensation, farmers would have no incentive to adapt the use to which they put their fields; they might even be induced to plant corn in the hopes of gaining compensation (curiously, this risk bears the technical name of "moral hazard"). As a result of the law, it is cows that stand in the fields and watch the trains go by.

In the same vein, a factory may spill dust, smoke or worse over the neighbouring area; if it were required to internalize those costs it might choose to close – or simply to move further afield, thereby requiring its workers to travel longer to work. Given the choice, the workers and their families may prefer to put up with the inconveniences.

The Polluter-Pays Principle

Considerations of those kinds led the OECD in 1972 to adopt the Polluter-Pays Principle. The name is misleading, because what it says is precisely that the polluter need not necessarily pay all the external costs resulting from its action.[9] The principle states:

> 4. The principle to be used for allocating costs of pollution prevention and control measures to encourage rational use of scarce environmental resources and to avoid distortions in... trade and investment is the so-called "Polluter-Pays Principle". The Principle means that the polluter should bear the expenses of carrying out the above-mentioned measures decided by public authorities to ensure that the environment is in an acceptable state.

A note on the implementation of the Polluter-Pays Principle, which accompanies the guiding principles just quoted, expands on the argument:

> 2. The Polluter-Pays Principle, as defined in paragraph 4 of the "Guiding Principles", states that the polluter should bear the expenses of preventing and controlling pollution "to ensure that the environment is in an acceptable state". The notion of an "acceptable state", decided by public authorities, implies that through a collective choice and with respect to the limited information available, the advantage of a further reduction in the residual social damage involved is considered as being smaller than the social cost of further prevention and control.

The key point for present purposes is "the notion of an 'acceptable state' *decided by public authorities*". In order to take into account the impact of economic decisions on third parties, the latter must be brought into the process. Without democratic political processes, the market cannot determine the prices which correspond to the costs and benefits of private transactions as perceived by those who are affected. It is not simply that the market cannot function fairly in isolation from politics; without the intervention of democratic processes the market will generate deceptive prices which distort the signals which the market communicates to buyers and sellers. Left to its own devices, the market will trip itself up in its own entanglements.

The name "Polluter-Pays Principle" is misleading on two counts. First, the polluter is actually the pair constituted of both the buyer and the seller. How the internalized external costs are allocated between those two depends on the shape of the corresponding supply and demand curves, or more generally of the bargaining power of each relative to the other. As the OECD "Note on the Implementation of the Polluter-Pays Principle" says:

> From the point of view of conformity with the Polluter-Pays Principle, it does not matter whether the polluter passes on to his prices some or all of the environmental costs or absorbs them.[10]

Secondly, the Polluter-Pays Principle concerns not only pollution, but the generation of any external environmental cost. In the interests of fairness in the workings of the market, it is indeed desirable to extend its application beyond that category defined by OECD to any external cost.

There is no corresponding principle for the internalization of external benefits, which is a pity. Nonetheless, a variety of subsidies paid by public authorities are in fact justified by that type of argument. Neo-liberals tend to decry them as market distortions; on the contrary, they bring prices closer to the costs and benefits as perceived by the community as a whole.

In short, once it is recognized that economic transactions involve not only buyers and sellers, but also all those who are affected whether they like it or not by the buyers' and sellers' activities, politics inevitably enter into the game. For Christian ethics it is inadmissible to ignore or exclude the third parties who are affected. The market cannot be fenced off from the rest of social activity.

The market economy thrives when the players are endowed with particular character traits. We shall concentrate on two of them here: the competitive spirit and individualism. They are closely related to each other. Each has its merits, provided it is bridled by the over-riding objective of the common good, and more specifically of the priority assigned to the poor.

The competitive spirit

The market economy prizes not just fighters, but winners. One of the roles of the market game is to clear the losers from the field. Social Darwinism is poles apart from Christian social ethics. The Bible states again and again that priority is due to the weak – the widow, the orphan, the foreigner.

> Cursed be he who makes the blind wander out of the way. And all the people shall say, Amen. Cursed be he who perverts the judgment of the stranger, fatherless, and widow. And all the people shall say, Amen. (Deut. 27:18-19)
>
> Lord, how long shall the wicked, how long shall the wicked triumph?... They slay the widow and the stranger, and murder the fatherless. (Ps. 94:3,6)

Many games are competitive. Not only can they be great fun, they can strengthen fellow-feeling between the adversaries – provided they keep the spirit of competition within the bounds of the game. If cooperation means working together for the common good, competition has its place within cooperation in so far as it reflects a shared activity furthering the shared objective. Society is endangered when the spirit escapes out of the game into other areas of human activity at the expense of different character traits which are more useful in those circumstances.

A harmonious world community assumes civilized competition. Competition implies rules, whether in personal life, in sports or in the economic realm. Unless controlled, competition degenerates into warfare and leads to the death or destruction of the loser.[11]

Individualism

The mathematical model of the market assumes that each individual's desires are independent of everyone else's desires. The contrary assumption, either that my pleasure resides in your happiness or conversely that I find my pleasure in my enemy's unhappiness, generates feedback loops beyond the model's technical capacity to handle. Convenience therefore rules out either alternative as a basis for comprehending market forces. This has two major disadvantages.

Above all, it is unrealistic. People's feelings actually often do depend on those of others. Marketing experts promoting the products of the firms which employ them show that they are well aware of that when they exploit people's tendency to "keep up with the Joneses", i.e. to want to buy something for the very reason that someone else whom they take as a role model has bought it (the dynamics of this tendency are more fully discussed in chapter 2).

While there are apologists so bogged down in the market ideology that they treat even gifts as exchanges of which the other half is postponed (the enduring influence of Marcel Mauss' work of 1924, *Essai sur le don*, is there to confirm this assertion), yet we all know that people often give presents because the pleasure the recipient feels makes the giver happy, too.

Schadenfreude (taking pleasure in the misfortunes of others) may be regrettable, but it is a character trait that assuredly exists. It undermines the foundations of the market as a theory as surely as do sympathy or altruism.

Secondly and to get around the drawback of unrealism, the defenders of the market ideology try to influence behaviour so as to bring it into line with the requirements of the theory, urging people to disregard their neighbour, i.e. to cultivate at best indifference and at worst selfishness. They do not however push their efforts so far as to threaten the urge to keep up with the Joneses, which is so very lucrative for them.

Individualism stands in tension with community. While neither should swamp the other, Christian social teaching stresses the importance of community. In the quotation below, Calvin reflects a wider range of Christian thought than merely the Reformed tradition:

> Just as the eye cannot do without the foot, the hand without the ear and the mouth without the stomach, likewise the great and the small cannot rest content with themselves but we must be united and have a mutual bond of fraternity... In short the communication of which St Paul talks here is that brotherly love which proceeds from the regard we have since God has joined us together and linked us like the members of a single body, and he wants each and every one of us to engage ourselves for our neighbours, that no one devote himself to his own particulars, but that we all serve in common. (Calvin on 1 Tim. 6:17-19)

Paul radically insists that we all are members of each other:

> For the body is not one member, but many. If the foot shall say, Because I am not the hand, I am not of the body; is it therefore not of the body? And if the ear shall say, Because I am not the eye, I am not of the body; is it therefore not of the body? If the whole body were an eye, where were the hearing? If the whole were hearing, where were the smelling? But now hath God set the members every one of them in the body, as it hath pleased him. And if they were all one member, where were the body? But now are they many members, yet but one body. And the eye cannot say unto the hand, I have no need of thee: nor again the head to the feet, I have no need of you. Nay, much more those members of the body, which seem to be more feeble, are necessary: And those members of the body, which we think to be less honourable, upon these we bestow more abundant honour; and our uncomely parts have more abundant comeliness. For our comely parts have no need: but God hath tempered the body together, having given more abundant honour to that part which lacked: That there should be no schism in the body; but that the members should have the same care one for another. And whether one member suffer, all the members suffer with it;

or one member be honoured, all the members rejoice with it. (1 Cor. 12:14-26)

James makes the same point by looking at community from the opposite side:

> If a brother or sister be naked, and destitute of daily food, and one of you say unto them, Depart in peace, be ye warmed and filled; notwithstanding ye give them not those things which are needful to the body; what doth it profit? (James 2:15-16)

It is not good enough to assume that by leaving everyone, particularly the poor and the weak, to look after themselves, everyone's needs will be met. The affirmative action of solidarity is indispensable.

All this is no more than putting into practice the injunction, "Thou shalt love the Lord thy God with all thy heart, and with all thy soul, and with all thy strength, and with all thy mind; and thy neighbour as thyself" (Luke 10:27). "The words 'as thyself' mean that one should love one's neighbour totally, 'with all one's heart'. It should not be read as a recommendation to love oneself first and afterwards or as well to love one's neighbour."[12]

The danger in the market ideology is its tendency to leave no space for community, but rather to praise individualism alone. The assumptions of the market theory are at odds not only with psychological reality, but also with the injunctions of Christian moral teaching.

2. Unto Every One Which Hath Shall Be Given

The market is not in perpetual equilibrium, solid and unmoving like a monument in the market square. It is constantly subject to shocks and shifts, as new products or methods of production are invented, as fashion or even the weather changes (people buy more cold drinks on a hot day). How does the market respond when it is knocked off balance? Is its equilibrium stable or unstable?

Stable equilibrium

The theory of the market prized by the neo-liberals claims that it is not only in stable equilibrium, but in a state of general equilibrium:

> In a competitive and decentralized market, the price system can achieve the mutual compatibility and the equilibrium of supply and demand on the market for every good and service.[1]

The neo-liberal model shows mathematically that a departure from equilibrium sets up automatic forces that bring the system back to equilibrium. Furthermore, the equilibrium is determinate: the final position is independent of the path taken towards equilibrium. The theory, originally elaborated by Léon Walras (1834-1910),[2] was later generalized and refined by Kenneth Arrow (Nobel Prize in economics 1972) and Gerard Debreu (Nobel Prize in economics 1983).

The model of general equilibrium, although unrealistic, remains at the heart of the analysis of economic problems. Most contemporary theories are founded on a relationship with general equilibrium – either because they accept it or because they oppose it. It is at the root of neo-classical economics which is today considered the dominant model.[3]

Walras was not taken in by his own scenario. He himself said that "this state of equilibrium is an ideal state, not a real one".

For the theory of stable equilibrium to work, two assumptions in particular must hold: there must be no externalities, and returns to scale must be constant or diminishing. We have seen in chapter 1 that the former does not hold: externalities are pervasive in the real world. We shall see later in this chapter that increasing returns are also widespread.

Returns are diminishing when it costs more to produce any given item of output than it cost to produce the previous one. This is the standard case presented in economics textbooks. The price rises along with the quantity of goods supplied because in a competitive economy the price which calls forth the supply is equal to the cost of producing the last unit.

When equilibrium prevails, everyone else charges the same price for the same product. Otherwise buyers would be abandoning the sellers asking a higher price in favour of those asking a lower one; that kind of movement is a form of disequilibrium. There are so many producers that no single one can influence the price, regardless of how much that particular producer offers for sale.

Now let us suppose that for some reason a customer asks the supplier for an extra item, thus increasing the total quantity sought on the market. The supplier of the last or marginal item can afford to supply an extra unit only at a higher price because it costs that much more to produce it.

On the other hand, other suppliers producing smaller quantities can afford to supply at a lower price, since for each producer the cost of producing the last item is lower in proportion to the smaller quantity being produced. One can conceive that a new producer will appear on the market who is willing to provide the item at an even lower price. Of course, at such a price the product will attract further customers and increase his output to satisfy them, but this will drive up costs. The problem will stop when the point is reached at which the cost of the last item produced equals the going price. Things will settle down at a new slightly higher price than before because of the increased demand, with each producer making the amount at which the cost of the last unit made equals that price.

Unstable equilibrium

Situations like the one just described may well occur in real life, but unstable equilibria also can be found. If the

equilibrium is unstable, any disturbance will lead to a movement away from the original position which will continue,
perhaps even at an accelerating pace, until the system breaks
down or some external obstacle forces it to a halt.

"Unto every one which hath shall be given; and from him
that hath not, even that which he hath shall be taken away
from him" (Luke 19:26 et par.) is an accurate description of
how the economy actually works, or at least decisive parts of
it. A joint report of the institute of social ethics of the Feder-
ation of Swiss Protestant churches and the Swiss justice and
peace commission of the Catholic church had this to say on
the subject:

> The social market economy... is founded on the conviction that
> a market freed from any social obligation cannot on its own
> ensure a socially acceptable distribution of wealth, but that it
> ends in the concentration of wealth in the hands of a few... At
> present the aspiration towards a free market, i.e. one separated
> from any social obligation, is again predominant.[4]

The following sections explain a number of the mechanisms through which the economy is subject to cumulative
processes, which in many cases are vicious circles.

INCREASING RETURNS TO SCALE

For any good or service, if the cost of production per unit
falls as the number of units produced rises, there are increasing returns to scale. They are widespread in the economy.
They are found wherever a heavy investment in overheads is
needed to begin production. Thus, to produce the first unit of
electricity from a hydroelectric dam or power plant is
extremely expensive, but to produce one more unit costs very
little. The phenomenon exists even with respect to the labour
of an individual person: most of the food a person consumes
simply goes to keep the body running. The extra amount of
food needed to make a special effort like doing one's job is
relatively small.

For the economy to achieve its ideal allocative efficiency,
the cost of producing an extra unit of output must equal the

extra revenue obtained by selling that unit – in formal terms, marginal cost must equal marginal revenue. If marginal cost falls with output, then to charge a uniform price corresponding to marginal cost will not cover the total cost of production; the heavy initial costs are not met. It is evident that this position of costs exceeding revenue cannot be sustained indefinitely in a free market where firms must earn a profit from their activities to survive. In such a case, the efficiency requirement would result in all the firms going out of business!

Each firm, however, sees a way out. Let us now suppose that a customer wishes to buy a further unit. Because its increased output lowers the cost of producing an extra unit, each supplier can now offer a lower price. Each will rush to accept the new demand before its competitors can. Indeed, without waiting for such an offer it will make every effort to attract one more customer than its competitors. Ideally, it will entice an existing customer away from them, thereby forcing the cost of its competitor's last unit up, increasing the gap between them. The loser of the initial fray is pushed into a position where it sells less and less as its cost of producing the last unit goes up and up. Meanwhile the winner of the skirmish increases its advantage as the amount it sells increases. The system rushes away from equilibrium.

Why should the producer do anything which appears so silly at first sight? After all, increasing its sales also increases its losses. We have already noted that the initial situation couldn't last anyway. The advantage of rushing into greater losses is that it forces the competitors into a position where they can sell less and less until in the end they disappear from the market. At that point competition has come to an end, and the winner has achieved monopoly. It can then fix its price wherever it likes in the light of whatever people are prepared to pay if pressed or coaxed. Such situations are common in the real world.

More fundamentally, someone must pay for the overheads or costs if the good or service is to be provided at all. Since even human labour is subject to increasing returns to scale, there can be no argument but that some at least of the goods and services produced under these conditions must be provided.

In an unregulated market such situations are likely to end spontaneously in a private monopoly. Should the seller be left free to seek to cover its overheads through the profit-maximizing techniques of monopoly pricing? The community can take various measures to protect the public interest against rapacious monopoly. A public or regulated monopoly can spread overheads over all the consumers by some method considered to be fair as an outcome of democratic political processes (see the section on the Polluter-Pays Principle in chapter 1); costs may be covered by the public at large through taxes, also determined by political processes. Examples of all these solutions can be found in the real world.

The community can regulate the industry while leaving it in private ownership or it can remove the sector from the market altogether. These kinds of measures, common in the recent past, are at present passing out of fashion, leaving the field free either to profit-maximizing monopolies or to industries engaged in a ruinous competitive race to the bottom at which lies the pot of gold labelled "monopoly".

THE TRIANGLE OF DESIRE

In chapter 1 we mentioned "keeping up with the Joneses". It is a relatively benign manifestation of a much more far-reaching phenomenon, close to the heart of the Christian faith. René Girard throws a revealing light on this deep-seated aspect of the human character and its implications.[5] Paul Dumouchel has drawn the implications of Girard's arguments for the workings of the economy.[6]

Scarcity is at the foundations of the economy. A definition of economics which was once current is "human behaviour as a relationship between given ends and scarce means which have alternative uses".[7] In this perspective, economics studies the efficient allocation of resources to reduce the gap between needs on the one hand and the quantity of goods and services available on the other. It is needs which determine the levels of production.

Girard, however, argues that we do not normally desire an object for its intrinsic characteristics. What we want is rather to imitate the person who has rendered the object desirable by appropriating it. Desire is a triangle. If more goods have been appropriated, desire, which is imitative, is thereby increased. Consequently, to produce more does not reduce the gap between what is needed and what is available; the gap remains intact. "He who loves silver will not be satisfied with silver; nor he that loves abundance with increase" (Eccl. 5:10).

Furthermore, we desire what another has in order that others will desire what we have; we also want to be role models. A cumulative process, a vicious circle, is thus set in motion. The process goes well beyond economics, to the very roots of violence. The role model whom we admire is at the same time a rival because he possesses what we want to possess. We have all seen children fighting over a toy. It is useless to try and end the fight by offering a similar toy to the child without one; he wants the very one which his role model has. In this psychological setting, it is not surprising if the imitator ends up destroying the role model in order to appropriate the desired object. "You are of your father the devil, and the lusts of your father you will do. He was a murderer from the beginning" (John 8:44). That having been achieved, he must then glorify the person he has destroyed, in order to preserve that person's status as a model worthy of imitation. The rival becomes the ideal of a model. "Your fathers killed the prophets and you build their sepulchres" (cf. Luke 11:47 and Matt. 23:29-30).

Expanded from the individual to the social level, in order to remove the role model/rival, society imputes to him its own evils, making him a scapegoat to be driven from its midst. Once this has been done society freed from its inherent rivalry can find its unity once more – "by his stripes we are healed" – ... until another role model/rival appears and the cycle starts off again.

> He is despised and rejected of men; a man of sorrows, and acquainted with grief... Surely he hath borne our griefs, and carried our sorrows: yet we did esteem him stricken, smitten of God, and afflicted. But he was wounded for our transgressions, he was bruised for our iniquities: the chastisement of our peace was upon him; and with his stripes we are healed. (Isa. 53:3-5)

Jesus was anxious to end this cycle once and for all. The ten commandments had already asserted the need to give up the urge to imitate through possession: "Thou shalt not covet" (Ex. 20:17) is an essential element in breaking the cycle.[8] Jesus went yet further by showing a role model free from grandeur, one who instead washed his companions' feet. In this as in the rest of his teaching he was realizing a message already present in the Old Testament: "He hath no form nor comeliness; and when we shall see him, there is no beauty that we should desire him" (Isa. 53:2).

The market economy as a model agrees with the tenth commandment since it claims that each need is autonomously determined. None the less, the marketing practices in the real market economy do exploit imitation and covetousness, thus placing stumbling blocks between us and the coming of the kingdom.

THE JUBILEE

The jubilee as presented in Leviticus 25 discerns the vicious cycles at work not only in the market economy, but in any unbridled economic system,[9] and shows how they can be dismantled. There are four elements in the jubilee:[10]

1) rest for the land
2) freedom for the slaves
3) cancellation of debts
4) return of the land to its original owners

They stand in turn on two foundations, reinstatement and the sabbath rest, but they, in their turn, constitute at root a single one: that of letting go.[11] They are each a way of neutralizing the vicious circle of the economy. Reinstatement acts by resetting the counters to zero, the sabbath rest by releasing the spring of action so that it no longer has the force to make the mechanism run.

The last three elements in the jubilee deal with a chain of events by which the poor are deprived even of the little they have. The scenario assumes a peasant family which in normal times can just make ends meet. Some mishap upsets the precarious balance: illness in the family, drought or bad weather... Since as a result the holding is unable to meet the family's needs, the family must borrow. However, in good times the holding could produce only enough to keep it going. Now, on top of current needs, it must meet the extra burden of repaying the debt. It falls inexorably further into debt. Unable to repay, it must part with some of its land. With even less land now, it no longer has any prospect of breaking even. When the family has consequently lost all its land, its only remaining recourse is to sell itself into slavery.

Beyond reinstating families on their land with their productive capacity intact, the jubilee aims to restore the entire just order of society. The jubilee message of Isaiah 61 enumerates several dimensions of this restoration: it is intended for the poor, the broken-hearted, the captives, the blind, the bruised (Luke 4:18). It will repair the damage done by the vicious cycles of the economy: "They shall raise up the former desolations, and they shall repair the waste cities, the desolations of many generations" (Isa. 61:4).

Of course, as long as the mechanism is in working order, once the counters have been reset to zero everything will start off again as before and sooner or later the operation will have to be repeated.

> [The] assumption is that things will go wrong if left alone. This is probably the most important single lesson we can derive from Leviticus. We should always assume that even if we set up the best system of rules we can devise, things will go wrong. People... will start to exploit one another, and some will seize the others' territory and amass wealth whilst others will get poor. So we must frame additional laws to put everything right every now and then, say every seven years, with a major clean-up once in fifty years, like the sabbatical and jubilee years.[12]

Deuteronomy recognizes the never-ending nature of the task when, at either end of the same passage concerning the seventh year, it states, "...there shall be no poor among you if you... observe all these commandments which I command you this day" (Deut. 15:4-5) but immediately afterwards, "For the poor shall never cease out of the land" (15:11) (this juxtaposition could of course alternatively be understood as a comment on humanity's inability to respect God's law).

The economy ceaselessly drives people, social classes, geographical regions, to its margins. The Bible repeatedly insists on the obligation to reach out and fetch them back. Calvin has this to say on the subject:

> God does not only want each of us to enjoy ourselves but wants our neighbours to share in the joy which is in us, and that we should not only invite, as a man, our wife; as a father, our children, but those who seem farther removed from us should be drawn to us and we should ask for them to be brought face to face with our God so that the most foreign and those most remote from us may share in our joy and experience the benefit of this – all the more so that this will take place all together, in line with Moses' words in this passage: that the strangers, widows and orphans should rejoice with those who present themselves to God in this way to make offerings to him. (on Deut. 16:13-17)

The jubilee as described in Leviticus is a rare and dramatic event, proclaimed by trumpets (Lev. 25:9). Such a theatrical presentation helps get the message across, but the essential purpose of the jubilee can be achieved at least as effectively by continuous action every day, by stubborn persistence.

The appropriate policy can be compared to the action of a kitchen mixer: it is constantly throwing the contents to the outer rim. It is necessary to bring it back all the time towards the centre. In that way the part stuck to the bowl is not always the same, it is constantly being replaced. This image suggests another way of accommodating to the truth enunciated in Deuteronomy 15:11: the poor may indeed never cease to be in need on the earth, but at least it need not always be the *same* poor. Justice can be constantly restored, even if at the very same time it is being injured. In any event

> the periodicity of the Sabbath and jubilee year is radicalized by Jesus and Paul by being focused on the eschatological now, or today. Any moment can become the year of God's favour... Now is the time of liberation, remission, forgiveness, reconciliation.[13]

Since the processes which generate the concentration of wealth and power on the one hand and impoverishment and exclusion on the other are cumulative, to curb the momentum as it gathers after the jubilee also contributes to restoration. The Pontifical Council for Justice and Peace applies this consideration to the practical question of the redistribution of land:

> Expropriation of land and its redistribution are only one aspect – and not the most complex one – of an equitable and effective policy of agrarian reform. In many cases, governments have not paid enough attention to providing areas subject to agrarian reform with the necessary infrastructures and social services, to setting up an efficient organization for technical assistance, to ensuring equitable access to credit at sustainable costs, to curbing distortions that favour large landholdings, and to fixing prices and forms of the farmers' payment for land that are compatible with what is needed for its development and with the living requirements of their families. Small farmers are often forced into debt. They then have to sell their rights and give up farming.[14]

THE SABBATH: GIVE THE ECONOMY A REST!

Leviticus 25 mentions only rest for the earth both when referring to the jubilee and to the sabbatical year. However, Exodus 23:9-12, which puts immediately next to each other the sabbatical year and the weekly sabbath, makes it clear that the rest concerns far more than the earth alone:

> Six days thou shalt do thy work, and on the seventh day thou shalt rest: that thine ox and thine ass may rest, and the son of thy handmaid, and the stranger, may be refreshed. (Ex. 23:12)

God himself gave the example by resting on the seventh day of the creation. Rest is an integral part of the cycle of creation.

One implication of the sabbath rest is to underline the importance of limiting one's wants. As Calvin says,

> We must rest completely, so that God can work in us; we must yield up our will, resign our heart, give up and abandon all the cupidity of our flesh... [The meaning of the sabbath] is not limited to just one day, but summons the whole course of our life. (commentary on Gen. 2:3)

Productivism is not part of the Bible's programme. The call to put all our strength into the service of God is in no way a call to produce as much as we possibly can. The emphatic insistence in the Old Testament on leaving gleanings makes that point:

> When thou cuttest down thine harvest in thy field, and hast forgot a sheaf in the field, thou shalt not go again to fetch it: it shall be for the stranger, for the fatherless, and for the widow: that the LORD thy God may bless thee in all the work of thine hands.
> When thou beatest thine olive tree, thou shalt not go over the boughs again: it shall be for the stranger, for the fatherless, and for the widow.
> When thou gatherest the grapes of thy vineyard, thou shalt not glean it afterward: it shall be for the stranger, for the fatherless, and for the widow.
> And thou shalt remember that thou wast a bondman in the land of Egypt: therefore I command thee to do this thing. (Deut. 24:19-22)

Verse 18 is even more emphatic than verse 22: "thou shalt remember that thou wast a bondman in Egypt, and the LORD thy God redeemed thee thence" – in other words you have passed the stage of being a slave, a tool whose entire purpose is production. Productivism, wanting to harvest absolutely everything, to let nothing go: these attitudes reduce the producer to a state of slavery.[15]

To insist on mastering and limiting one's wants may seem especially utopian at a time when *la pensée unique* ("the single economic thought", or "TINA – There Is No Alternative") is levelling the playing fields so that only market games can be played on them, when the struggle for survival forces the marginalized to cling at any cost to the dominant economy, when the official doctrine of work-fare opens the way at best to "MacJobs". Yet control over one's desires is an unbeatable counterforce to the vicious cycles driven by greed.

We return to this subject, but from a different vantage point, in chapter 3. This section has concentrated on the importance of limiting wants from what economists call the supply side; chapter 3 deals with the issue from the demand side, the urge to consume.

3. The Limits of the Market

They were thy merchants: they traded the persons of men and vessels of brass in thy market. (Ezek. 27:13)

The outer limits of the market

IS IT LICIT TO BUY AND SELL ANYTHING WHICH CAN BE BOUGHT AND SOLD?

There are a number of goods and services which have all the characteristics which make them easy to buy and sell, but which people feel ought not to be exposed to the laws of the market: human organs or surrogate mothers (womb-renting), for instance. In some places it is considered indecent to buy human blood from people, while it is bought and sold in others. (Part of the objection to treating blood as marketable is that it is often poor or otherwise vulnerable people who accept to sell their blood. In these circumstances the exchange violates the principles of freedom and equality which commutative justice demands – see chapter 6.) The drug trade is basically illegal, but trade in other addictive substances like tobacco is not. (One of the objections to selling addictive substances is again that the buyers, being addicted, are not free partners. Consuming drugs other than tobacco, however, seems to arouse stronger objections having nothing to do with justice but involving norms of correct behaviour.) One can find economists who argue that there is nothing wrong with blackmail, for instance when it amounts to being paid for the service of keeping a secret.

In short, every society recognizes that there are limits to what it is licit to trade on the market. Different societies may put these limits in different places, and for a given society the limits may move over time.

SOLDIERS IN THE MARKET: MERCENARY SERVICE

Whether military service is one which can be bought and sold like any other has long aroused contending feelings. The 16th-century Zürich reformer Zwingli was opposed to mercenary service, which was a major source of employment and income in Switzerland in his time.[1] The debate about the legitimacy of private armies is still active today. The United Nations Human Rights Commission adopted a resolution in April 2002 which "reaffirm[ed] that the use of mercenaries and their recruitment, financing and training are causes for grave concern to all states and violate the purposes and principles enshrined in the charter of the United Nations" (Res. 2002/5). It was however adopted by 36 votes to 8 with 9 abstentions. Most of the countries which are home to firms which supply mercenary services either voted against the resolution or abstained.[2]

International trade in labour

Migration raises some interesting questions about the outer limits of the market. The labour market is very much part of the market economy. It is generally accepted that each worker should be free to seek the job which suits him or her best and that employers should compete in the market for the labour they need. The free market encourages employers to use labour effectively and encourages workers to move to jobs which are more satisfying and better paid. Mobility is an essential characteristic of the labour market and willingness to move is considered a virtue.

The Quaker James Hack Tuke used this point of view in defending the humanitarian objective of relieving the misery of the impoverished Irish during the great famine in the middle of the 19th century:

> Surely if any of the so-called "leaders of the people" of Ireland had any article to dispose of, at present valueless in Ireland, but priceless in America, they would not hesitate to transfer or take it there. To them "Ireland for the Irish" would then indeed be deemed a meaningless cry. But is it less meaningless when that article is labour, and the alternatives beggary, or independence and comfort?... Just as well might they oppose the exportation of the thousands of tons of Irish potatoes now leaving for New York, and proclaim that they should be left to rot at home.[3]

Notwithstanding this impeccable market ideology, it is difficult to find a country anywhere in the world which does not set strict limits on immigration. There is strong popular support for preventing the labour market from working freely. As the African economist Samir Amin has said,

> The litany of the market cure, invoked at every turn, comes to a dead halt here. To suggest that in a henceforth unified world, human beings, commodities and capital should be at home everywhere is quite simply unacceptable. The most fanatical partisans of the free market suddenly find at this point an argument for the protectionism that they fustigate elsewhere as a matter of principle.[4]

Various arguments are used to defend this limitation of the market. In rich countries, one argument is that if workers from low-wage areas were free to enter in search of higher paid work, the high wages of workers already there could be pressed down. But there are arguments against that one. Even if wages fell, so would the costs and prices of goods; there would thus be other people as well as the immigrant workers who benefit, just as there are people who lose: it is necessary to examine the case carefully before passing judgment. Furthermore, the Bible is perfectly clear about the over-riding priority due to the poor. It in no way defends protecting the high earnings of the rich at the expense of the urgent needs of the poor. In the words of the Magnificat: "He hath filled the hungry with good things; and the rich he hath sent empty away" (Luke 1:53).

The liberalization of trade in certain categories of labour is, however, an issue in the negotiation of a General Agreement on Trade in Services (GATS) under the auspices of the World Trade Organization (WTO).[5] The rich countries are anxious to facilitate their access to highly qualified people from poor countries, "e.g. auditors, physicians, teachers, etc."[6] while continuing to place obstacles in the way of simple workers. The qualified people are often more urgently needed in their own country, even if it cannot offer salaries as high as the rich countries. Furthermore, the source country has usually incurred the costs of educating these people.

Their departure deprives the country of the return on its investment, while conversely the country of destination benefits from the skills without having to pay for their production.

The example of international trade in labour confirms that the powerful see the market as a tool at their service which they readily discard when its logic points in a different direction.

The cultural exception

Another argument against migration is that it upsets the local culture. In this respect, the urge to restrict migration can be linked to the debate in the context of the World Trade Organization concerning "the cultural exception". The defenders of this exception – led in particular by France – argue that international trade in products of the media industry should be regulated to protect local cultures: "As a doctrine (it does not have any legal status, nor does it exist as such in any agreement or treaty), the 'cultural exception' is based on the principle that culture is not like any other merchandise because it goes beyond the commercial: cultural goods and services convey ideas, values and ways of life which reflect the plural identities of a country and the creative diversity of its citizens."[7]

THE RESPECTIVE REALMS OF POLITICS AND THE MARKET

It is widely considered improper to buy votes. Political democracy is supposed to ensure that those who have little sway in the market can nonetheless make themselves felt. It is intended precisely to provide a different structure of power to serve as a counter-weight to the power of the market.

On the other hand, hardly anyone disputes that there is a sphere within which the market can be left to function on its own. Political processes canalize the market in a variety of ways, for instance:

- They serve to repress abuses in the market: chapter 4 explores this question.
- They can provide a supportive framework for the market, establishing rules and regulations to ensure that it works

smoothly. Inescapably, they also strive to ensure that it works in the interests of those who make the rules: hence the importance of establishing, within the political system, who the rule-makers are, and in particular to avoid duplicating the power structures of the market economy.

- They set the outer limits to the market, deciding what may or may not be bought and sold in the market.
- They take some of the decisions which will not be left to the market because they are subject to a different logic, for instance a logic of symbolism, solidarity or gratuitousness (other decisions of this kind are left to private organizations like charities).

Since the balance of power is often different in the market and in the political domain, the one can be called in to rectify imbalances in the other. But the two domains cannot be neatly separated.

Laws are drawn up through political processes. Legislators sometimes seek intentionally to serve their private interests. Whatever the means by which they entered the legislature, whether democratic or not, they represent some sort of constituency, and it is undoubtedly their duty to defend their constituency's interests. If however they are paid by their constituency or by some other interest, say a company – rather than by the collectivity as a whole – then the market has entered into the political process.

Even if the legislators are perfectly public-spirited, they can only act in accordance with their understanding. In many countries the law discriminates systematically against those whose property rights and obligations are defined in a social system different from that of the market – indigenous peoples for instance – simply because the legislators are unfamiliar with the workings of other forms of social organization. Hence the importance of ensuring participation in the political processes by all the cultures present in the territory. The issue of participatory democracy to complement representative democracy is attracting growing attention. The European Union is seriously concerned about this issue.[8] The World Bank insists that it is a valuable feature of the process of preparing Poverty Reduction Strategy Papers, in which it presses its debtor countries to engage; according to the experience of some churches in poor countries, there is still a long way to go before practice corresponds to the ideal which the World Bank proclaims.

The respective realms of the judicial system and the market

Most of us, like Amos, disapprove of judges who sell the righteous for silver and the poor for a pair of shoes (Amos 2:6). That is a particularly obvious intervention of the market in the judicial system, but there are other more subtle yet pervasive ways in which market considerations influence its workings.

In many societies, it is generally argued that one of the tasks of justice is to protect the weak against the strong. Yet judicial proceedings are costly and demand technical knowledge about the law and its workings, which can and sometimes has to be bought in the market. A financially solid party to judicial proceedings can frighten off the weaker party by the mere threat of costs to come. Even in democracies, large corporations use their financial might in this way to intimidate for instance the press or academic researchers who criticize their activities, not to mention civic society organizations which oppose their interests.

Secondly, legal proceedings can be time-consuming. Since the poor cannot wait, drawing the proceedings out gives the advantage to the wealthier party. Any worker who takes his employer or former employer to court can confirm that.

All the above are examples of ways in which the judicial system can become ensnared in market logic.

LIMITS TO WANTS

One of the outcomes of the market as it really exists is to multiply wants. The most important outer limit to the market is precisely the limit to wants. While this section concentrates on wants from what economists call the demand side, chapter 2 deals with the issue from the supply side, the urge to produce.

> From whence come wars and fightings among you? Come they not hence, even of your lusts that war in your members? Ye lust, and have not: ye kill, and desire to have, and cannot obtain: ye fight and war, yet ye have not, because ye ask not. Ye ask, and receive not, because ye ask amiss, that ye may consume it upon your lusts. (James 4:1-3)

This has long been a constant of economic ethics in the Reformed tradition. As Calvin said, "Let us not strive for more than is required by the needs of this present life. For nature is satisfied with little; and everything which is above natural need is superfluous." The remark was inspired by a passage in 1 Timothy:

> Perverse disputings of men of corrupt minds, and destitute of the truth, supposing that gain is godliness: from such withdraw thyself. But godliness with contentment is great gain. (1 Tim. 6:5-6)

The sumptuary laws introduced in Geneva during Calvin's time rested on ethical considerations, but admittedly as part of a complex set of reasons which included political and economic constraints as well. The simplicity of dress and manners of the Puritans and Quakers in the 17th century and later rested more firmly, but still not entirely, on ethical grounds.

The World Council of Churches has reiterated the question, without separating spiritual from social and ecological concerns:

> Just as humanity has more or less developed a sense for a required minimum of consumption to ensure a decent life, so we should be considering where maximum limits may lie, and how those might be implemented before excess leads to ruin.[9]

The Puritans held that economic success was a sign of the grace of God. This becomes a dangerous deviation when it accepts private prosperity without afterthought, in particular without thought for God's intention for the use of riches. Referring to 2 Corinthians 8:15, which in turn quotes the passage in Exodus concerning manna – "And when they did mete it with an omer, he that gathered much had nothing over, and he that gathered little had no lack" – Calvin says,

> We do not now have an omer or other fixed measure ordained by God, according to which we must deal out the provisions of each day; but we are commanded to live soberly and with temperance and forbidden to debauch ourselves if we should happen to experience abundance. That is why those who have riches... should take note that abundance is not destined to intemperance or dissolution, but to meet the needs of the brothers [and sisters].

Elsewhere he says,

> So here is the condition under which God puts wealth in the hands of the rich: it is in order that they may have the occasion and the means also to meet the needs of their neighbours who are indigent. (on Deut. 24:19-22)

A further aspect of the desirability of limiting wants can be mentioned here. One of the results of the market is to stimulate new technology. If, however, the innovation simply renders goods obsolete which are still perfectly serviceable, the progress consists in a benefit to the sellers of the new goods at the expense of a loss to the owners of the previous ones. Society is not automatically better off. If the production of obsolescence also results in greater demands for the scarce resources of the environment which are particularly important to the poor for meeting their immediate needs, the merit is even more dubious.

The inner limits of the market

To set the outer limits to the market, a catalogue may be drawn up of the goods and services which it is not licit to trade, and the quantities traded may be weighed. The inner limits concern not what is traded, but how it is traded.

DISHONESTY

Dishonesty is undoubtedly the most obvious of the inner limits to the market. The Old Testament inveighs repeatedly against traders who use dishonest weights and measures –

"[making] the ephah small and the shekel great and falsifying balances by deceit" (Amos 8:5) or misdescribing goods – "selling the refuse of the wheat" (Amos 8:6). The scope for fraud has grown with the increasing sophistication of the economy. Twenty-three centuries after Amos, Calvin asked, "If in those days God had to repress dishonesty with respect to weights and measures, what about today?" (on Deut. 25:13-19). If it was so in the relatively simple trading economy of 16th-century Geneva, what about the still more complex trading and service economy of Geneva (or elsewhere) now?

Contracts

It is dishonest not to respect contracts. As Zwingli said:

> Concerning the debt contracted on the occasion of a fair bargain of purchase or sale, there exists, God wish it so, no Christian who would claim that he should not settle or honour what he has promised and in respect of which he has received a corresponding object in exchange. Anyone who defended that opinion would be a thief ... To talk of contracts ... would take us too far afield. This kind of debt must be honoured before God and before men.[10]

It should be stressed that the foregoing concerns fair bargains of purchase or sale. In the first place it must be fair, as Zwingli also said, "In so far as cheating with respect to a purchase has been discovered, the authorities know how to demand compensation."[11] Secondly, it concerns a transaction between parties both of whom have the appropriate independence and means.

It follows that one should not make commitments one is not sure to be able to meet, and therefore in particular one should not over-extend one's business or incur debts in the hopes that a speculative gain will cover them. The resounding recent failures of property speculators, banks and business tycoons, or the dramatic shortfalls and shortcomings of pension funds, should serve to bring this moral principle back to the fore. Honest savers have lost savings they entrusted to those institutions, and taxpayers are being required more or less indirectly to bail out the victims.

Enterprise involves risk. Any venture can fail. There may indeed be sense in encouraging people to take risks with what is their own. It is more difficult to defend risking what belongs to other people, especially if they are not knowing and willing partners in the venture. In the United States, bankruptcy law is lenient in order to encourage the spirit of enterprise. On the other hand, British law now requires that an enterprise conduct its affairs in such a way that it can cease business at any time and have sufficient assets to cover its liabilities.

SPECULATION

The market serves its purpose of allocating resources efficiently in so far as prices correspond to costs and costs correspond to the benefits which society foregoes when it decides to use the resource in one particular way rather than another. (The benefit foregone when a resource is denied to one use but put to another is what economists call the "opportunity cost".)

With speculation, prices depend not on costs, but on what speculators think the price will be next. Speculation is a form of gambling in that one player wins what the other loses, minus the payment to the casino or broker for services rendered. There is a Quaker statement which sums up the traditional Protestant view of speculation:

> Gambling by risking money haphazardly disregards our belief that possessions are a trust. The persistent appeal to covetousness... is fundamentally opposed to the unselfishness which was taught by Jesus Christ and by the New Testament as a whole. The attempt, which is inseparable from gambling, to make profit out of the inevitable loss and possible suffering of others is the antithesis of that love of one's neighbour on which our Lord insisted. Moreover, we must consider the moral and spiritual plight of those who by indulgence in gambling become suddenly possessed of large financial resources for which they have rendered no service to the community.[12]

Apart from the moral dangers to which that passage refers, speculation interferes with the workings of the real economy. The coffee on which speculators speculate is the same coffee which many of us drink. Six out of every seven dollars spent on coffee represent speculative transactions rather than ones related to those who want to process or consume the product. The price we pay for our coffee does not correspond to the real cost of supplying it, but to the bets of gamblers. Fair trade coffee, which is now sold in many West European supermarkets, is an attempt to protect coffee growers from that kind of thing (for more information on fair trade, see www.fairtrade.net).

The trouble is that a clear line cannot technically be drawn between whether a transaction has occurred for speculative or productive purposes. Ethically, the situation is like that of the just price: the criterion is whether the transaction expresses the love of one's neighbour.

MONOPOLY AND HOARDING

People who have power, including the power which money confers, can acquire goods and withhold them from the market in order to force up the price for their private benefit. Calvin speaks of "those who, facing high prices, keep their granaries closed; it's as if they cut the throats of the poor when they reduce them to hunger in this way". Indeed they do, since the poor have no supplies in their larder, unlike the rich who can afford to hoard. Besides, hoarding pushes prices out of line with costs.

Monopoly also involves a divergence between price and cost. Economic theory can prove this mathematically, but the theory has the drawback of resting on assumptions which do a poor job of describing economic reality. A more robust explanation is that in a transaction involving a monopoly, one party has much more power than the other. The more powerful party – the monopoly – can abuse its position and charge a higher price than costs justify. The remedy consists in reducing the inequality. One method is to weaken the stronger party, e.g. by breaking it up or encouraging competitors. This corresponds to the policy of the European Union or the United States against monopolies and cartels.

Another method is to strengthen the other party to the transaction so that it can negotiate on more equal terms. The trade-union movement and collective bargaining constitute an important example.

Some monopolies are inevitable in that technical constraints make it uneconomic to have several competing suppliers on the market. Historically this has been the case with railways, electricity supply or water, for instance. One way of dealing with this type of situation has been either to regulate the monopoly or to put it in public ownership. Either way, political power is used in an effort to counterbalance economic power. With the rise of the market ideology, this type of solution is increasingly contested. Privatization, deregulation and other such policies are leaving monopolies freer to behave like monopolies.

The existence of increasing returns to scale opens the door to monopoly (see pp.20-22). Whichever enterprise can increase its production to a greater extent enjoys lower costs and can therefore sell at a price lower than competitors can meet. In these circumstances, whoever gets a head start for whatever reason can drive competitors out of business and establish a monopoly.

EXPLOITATION

Marxism may have collapsed as a political system in Central and Eastern Europe but exploitation, which inspired Marx in the first place, has not vanished. Exploitation is in a sense the mirror image of the just price. The *Concise Oxford English Dictionary* defines "exploit" as "to utilize for one's own ends, treat selfishly as mere workable material (persons, etc.)". It reflects absence of love for one's neighbour. The wage which the market determines may be unfair if the market is unequal. The love of one's neighbour calls for a correction to the logic of the market. This is one of the lessons to be drawn from the parable of the workers in the vineyard (Matt. 20:1-14). It reminds us to look at the wage from the point of view of the unemployed worker rather than from that of the yield to the employer:

A householder went out early in the morning to hire labourers
into his vineyard. When he had agreed with the labourers for a
penny a day, he sent them into his vineyard. And he went out
about the third hour, and saw others standing idle in the mar-
ketplace, and said unto them; Go ye also into the vineyard, and
whatsoever is right I will give you. And they went their way.
Again he went out about the sixth and ninth hour, and did like-
wise. And about the eleventh hour he went out, and found
others standing idle, and said unto them, Why stand ye here all
the day idle ? They said to him, Because no man hath hired us.
He saith unto them, Go ye also into the vineyard; and whatsoever is right, that shall ye receive. So when evening had come,
the lord of the vineyard said to his steward, Call the labourers,
and give them their hire, beginning from the last unto the first.
And when they came that were hired about the eleventh hour,
they received every man a penny. But when the first came, they
supposed that they should have received more; and they like-
wise received every man a penny. When they had received it,
they murmured against the goodman of the house, saying,
These last have worked only one hour, and thou hast made them
equal unto us, which have borne the burden and heat of the day.
But he answered one of them, and said, Friend, I do thee no
wrong: didst not thou agree with me for a penny? Take that
thine is, and go thy way: I will give unto this last, even as unto
thee.

EXTERNALITIES

A transaction in the market takes place between a buyer
and a seller (see pp. 11-12). The operation behind the transaction may, however, involve further people regardless of
whether they like it or not. The third parties may enjoy benefits or suffer costs. Water warmed by a nuclear power plant
on the sea coast makes it possible for neighbours to raise oys-
ters: this is an environmental benefit. Radiation released by a
nuclear facility increases the incidence of leukaemia in the
neighbourhood: this is an environmental and social cost.
Since externalities are costs or benefits which accrue neither
to the buyers nor to the sellers, they are at best likely to be
ignored by the parties to the transaction. Market prices which
do not reflect externalities thus give misleading signals

which in turn lead to inefficiency in the economy. Furthermore, there are few transactions which do not involve externalities.

But there is worse. Buyers and sellers actually share an interest in externalizing costs to the greatest extent possible. Why pay yourself if you can make other people pay instead? Furthermore, whereas an economic transaction normally takes place between a limited number of identifiable partners, externalities may affect a larger number of people more difficult to identify. If those affected are scattered and perhaps unaware of what is happening to them, they are more likely to have to carry external costs or forgo external benefits. Externalities often bring into play relationships between the strong and well organized on the one hand and the weak or poorly organized on the other. Collective organization or official intervention is normally required to rectify externalities.

Collective goods

Collective goods are those which are available for everyone if they are available for anyone: a public park, for instance (see pp.9-11). The market cannot establish a price corresponding to the demand for goods of this kind because it is in the interests of each person to pretend to attach little value to it in the hope that someone else will pay for it instead. That is why collective goods are normally provided by public authorities, who meet the cost through compulsory payments like taxes.

If the market is allowed to invade the provision of collective goods, one builds a society of private affluence and public squalor, to quote the United States economist J.K. Galbraith. Or, as Calvin said, "there are people so greedy and malicious as to be upset that they have to share the sun and air with others" (on James 5:2).

4. The Convenience of the Market

Preconditions for the market to play its proper social role

The market certainly has advantages as a convenient way of dealing with a wide range of economic problems, but it is not a panacea for them.

The World Business Council for Sustainable Development, composed in November 2003 of 170 major corporations, was established as part of the vast process of reflection which led up to the United Nations Conference on Environment and Development, in Rio de Janeiro in June 1992 (for more information see its web site www.wbcsd.ch). The then chairman of the Business Council, the Swiss industrialist Stephan Schmidheiny, published a paper containing an enthusiastic if rather jumbled catalogue of advantages of the market. In order to analyze and assess both the strengths and the weaknesses of the market, we shall present this passage and then comment on some of the points it makes.

THE VIRTUES OF THE MARKET[1]

The market does not tell us where to go, but it provides the most efficient means of getting there. Therefore, society – through its political systems – will have to make value judgments, set long-term objectives...

Open markets (1) can motivate people... When resources are priced properly (2), the pursuit of competitiveness encourages producers to minimize resource use (3)... The competition (4) inherent in open markets is the primary driving force for the creation of new technology (5). And new technology is needed to use resources more efficiently...

Open, competitive markets create jobs (6) and opportunities (7), and thus are the most effective way of meeting people's needs (8). Accessible markets empower (9) people, and offer the greatest opportunities to the poor (10). Free markets are also inseparable from the other forms of freedom (11) sweeping the planet at the close of the 20th century...

> But the fall of communism does not represent the total victory of capitalism. It is merely the end of a system that, as practised in Eastern Europe and the Soviet Union, reflected neither economic nor environmental truths. This should encourage those of us who believe in the efficacy of the market-place to eliminate its failures and weaknesses and to build on its strengths.
>
> (The numbers in brackets are references to points explored below.)

The market does not automatically ensure that the economy will meet the needs of society fairly. If the market is to serve this purpose, it must satisfy a certain number of conditions.

It must be open and competitive (1,4). We have seen that in order to be competitive, the market must be composed of several buyers and several sellers, not too unequal in power.

OPENNESS

If the market is open (1), the constant threat that new actors may appear keeps everyone on their toes. It also encourages them to behave in such a way that excessive profits or obviously inefficient methods do not serve as bait to attract new actors.

Open markets imply not only that one is free to enter them, but also to leave them. Buyers and sellers must be free to refuse to buy or sell if they wish. Freedom to withdraw from the market often fails to get the attention it requires. The neo-liberal penchant for work-fare, which restricts the freedom of people to withdraw from the labour market (10), increases the power of buyers of labour services relative to sellers, weakening the position of people who are already weak.

Nor can the poor put off buying what they need, since they have no reserves. They are consequently vulnerable to the wealthy who can impose their conditions, having reserves and thus the means to wait. Calvin denounces the behaviour of the rich in these circumstances:

> [Amos] speaks of the greed of the rich, who in times of scarcity stand as if they had their foot on the throat of the poor people and reduce them to a state like slavery. For we know what indigence and extreme need lead to. When people are pressed by famine, they would sell their lives a hundred times in order to redeem their hunger, whatever the price might be. (on 4:1)

The market works best when it is just a game, dealing with non-essentials, rather than when the very lives of the actors are at stake (8).

Apart from freedom to enter and leave the market, to stay in it or outside it, the agents in the market, as people, have a responsibility to remain open to those who have no access to the market either because they have nothing marketable to sell or because they do not have the means – most immediately, the money – to buy what is available in the market. It is to this kind of openness that Deuteronomy refers when it calls on us to open our hand:

> For the poor shall never cease out of the land: therefore I command thee, saying, Thou shalt open thine hand wide unto thy brother [and sister], to thy poor, and to thy needy, in thy land. (Deut. 15:11)

Calvin commented on this passage:

> It is not without cause that God commands those who have the means, to open their hand to succour the poor and hungry in the land; as if [the passage] said that God puts before our eyes how he wants to be served by us: that we render as tribute to him the goods which he has provided to us in such abundance; indeed he sends us the poor as his receivers. The alms are given to mortal creatures, ... but with respect to God it is homage of the goods which he has given us and for which we are indebted to him. (on Deut. 45:11-15)

By specifying that Deuteronomy 15:11 concerns alms – which are essentially a non-market transaction – Calvin underlines that the passage is calling on us to break free from the compound of the playing field and to reach out to those who are unable to play.

INFORMATION

Another precondition for the market to work fairly is that information should be easily available (this precondition is not explicitly mentioned in the passage quoted in the box at the beginning of the chapter, but it is no less important for that). Buyers and sellers should be able to compare prices; information on the nature and quality of goods or services offered for sale should be readily available. At this same elementary level of information, the quantity offered for a given price should be easy to ascertain.

Increasingly, buyers want to know not only about the product, but also about how it was produced. An important fringe of consumers want to know what the impact of the production process is on the health and safety of the workers or other people affected or on the environment. They may want to know whether the workers are fairly treated. Yet in the WTO the United States argues that to oblige sellers to inform buyers about the nature of what they are buying constitutes an obstacle to trade and should be forbidden under WTO rules. It is in other words arguing that the market depends on the ignorance of buyers to function: there is according to this view nothing wrong with foisting the refuse on consumers as if it were wheat (Amos 8:6).

Easy access to information involves free expression, the freedom for different points of view to contend with each other. The same freedom lies at the root of democracy. It is only if people who notice what is going on can complain that remedial steps are likely to be taken. The market and democracy share a number of preconditions.

FREEDOM

Free markets are inseparable from other forms of freedom (11). If the market is to work properly, participants must be free to take their own decisions on the basis of what is on offer and at which prices. They must be free to refuse to buy, free to complain, free to offer a new product, service or way of doing things. They must be free from domination. If these conditions are met, one of the main advantages and resource-saving functions of the market can come into play: it decentralizes decisions. The multiplicity of participants, each pursuing its own particular interest, helps to fashion an overall economy which, if all the preconditions are met, serves the collective interest of the participants. As the grandfather of economics, Adam Smith (1723-90) said, the individual

> neither intends to promote the public interest, nor knows how much he is promoting it... He intends only his own gain, and he is... led by an invisible hand to promote an end which was no part of his intention.[2]

Freedom, however, requires a reasonable degree of equality between participants. Trade between unequals, and especially between parties one of whom is dependent on the other, may ill serve the public interest. But what about a world in which huge corporations have their spokesmen in the legislature and through their advertising budgets influence not only the demand for particular goods and services but also the editorial content of the media?

"Between the strong and the weak, freedom oppresses and it is the law which frees," said Jean-Jacques Rousseau in *The Social Contract*.

EMPOWERMENT

The decentralized decision-making implicit in the market is supposed to empower people (9). By leaving them responsible for their own decisions, it provides a convenient means of organizing and exploiting the vast quantity of information needed if the whole gamut of goods and services demanded by society is to be met. Open markets empower people who discover new challenges and opportunities to take advantage of their discoveries. It does not always work in that way, however. Sometimes the people it claims to empower are more like motorists trapped in traffic jams, the result of their decentralized decision-making.

Anyway, some other neo-liberal economists as keen to vaunt the marvels of the market disagree with Schmidheiny on empowerment. On the contrary, they argue, the market is all-powerful; therefore, it leaves no room for empowerment. "You cannot buck the Market," said Margaret Thatcher, then prime minister of the United Kingdom, in 1988, in such a way that you could almost hear the capital M. It was also she who applied the phrase "There Is No Alternative" to the market, thus earning the nickname TINA.

In any event, the preconditions for empowerment are not always met. In the last paragraph of the passage quoted in the box, Schmidheiny recognizes that the market is itself in competition with other ways of organizing the economy. Those who believe in its efficacy must strive to eliminate its failures and weaknesses. There will be cases where non-market mechanisms offer a more effective solution. As he says, "We need to ascertain where regulations work best and how they may be complemented by economic instruments and by self-regulation to form an optimal mix."[3] There exist alternatives to the market for achieving specific objectives. The choice between these methods can be made not only on equity grounds but also on those of efficiency.

Useful consequences of the market, if it is working properly

Supply and demand meet in the market. Any market will determine some sort of price. If the market is to serve the common good, however, goods and services must be priced properly (2). What counts as a just price is a problem which already worried Thomas Aquinas in the 13th century. The issues which preoccupied him are still with us (see chap. 8). Environmental concerns, in particular the externalities discussed in chapter 1, complicate them still further.

The competitive economy encourages producers to keep an eye on costs. If a competitor can produce a good or service equally satisfactorily to consumers at lower cost, it gains an advantage. Competition encourages care in the cost of production. However, the market responds directly to costs, and to resource use only through costs. The ways to minimize one's costs also include exploiting others, externalizing costs by imposing them on others or taking advantage of open access to collective goods to "ride free" at the expense of others. In so far as economic agents, be they producers or consumers, resort to any of these devices, the market economy fails to minimize resource use (3).

At best, competitors take prices as set. But they are set by the existing legal system, and by demand which is in turn set by the existing distribution of income. In short, the competitor accepts the existing power relationships in society, however just or unjust they may be.

What the market unassisted cannot do

Meet the whole range of people's independent needs

Open, competitive markets are the most effective way of meeting people's needs (8), according to the box. The needs which the market is equipped to meet are those which the economy can satisfy. These are only a part of human needs.

Behind the conclusion that open, competitive markets meet people's needs hides the assumption that people have these needs independently of the market, which simply brings the consumers together with suppliers able to provide what they need. This requires some preconditions more demanding than those enumerated in the box.

In particular, supply must be assured solely by firms so small that they cannot individually influence what consumers in general want. Relations between buyers and sellers need to be impersonal and at arm's length, the buyer simply looking for the seller who can supply at the lowest cost what the buyer has determined to be what he needs. In this scenario, the opportunities (7) which the market offers are opportunities to meet independently determined needs more effectively.

On the other hand, the market as it really exists is dominated by firms so large that consumers cannot deal with them on equal terms. If equality exists, it is between large organizations – firms, governments, trade unions and maybe consumers' associations.[4] Firms have the capacity to influence consumers and in particular to create new needs. The invention of new technology (5) serves not only to use resources more efficiently, but also to invent new goods and services, new wants – thereby expanding demand and pressure on resources (3).

In so far as producers instigate the needs they satisfy, albeit efficiently, an ethical question arises: What is the merit in meeting such needs?

MEET THE NEEDS OF THE POOR

The needs which the market meets are those which are expressed by demand in the market. The public votes by its expenditure: not one person-one vote, but one dollar-one vote. The rich have more votes than the poor (10). The market's preferential option is for the rich. In terms of Rawlsian justice, this is not necessarily faulty:[5] in so far as the rich make the investments on which the livelihood of the poor depend, the method can be effective. All the more so if the rich capitalists are inspired by the Protestant ethic to invest in order to provide a decent livelihood for the poor. If, on the other hand, the rich invest what they do not spend on consumption in activities which meet their own needs in preference to those of the poor, the Rawlsian condition is not met.

They are all the more likely to make this latter choice in that it is more profitable. The market is not equipped to tackle the problem of distributive justice (see chapter 6). The distribution it generates ineluctably favours the rich.

It follows that the market needs to be counterbalanced by another system in which people rather than dollars have equal weight, i.e. a participatory political system. The political system must set the limits to the market (see chapter 3).

PROVIDE A JOB FOR EVERYONE WHO WANTS ONE

"Open, competitive markets create jobs" (6). Jobs are certainly important, a need, not just as a source of income, but also as a source of dignity if not identity.

Any productive system creates jobs. The question is, does it produce the number – not to mention the kind – of jobs society wants? The British economist John Maynard Keynes

(1883-1946) established that the market economy could ensure full employment, provided it was combined with management by the government of the overall level of demand – what is now called macro-economic policy. Keynesian management worked well for several decades. Without macro-economic management by the government, the market will generate the number of jobs needed to meet the spontaneous demand for goods and services. Except by the purest chance, this will leave a proportion of the population unemployed, which is in fact exactly what the market economy left to itself normally does. The opposite situation, in which the resulting overall demand for labour is greater than the available supply, resulting in inflation, can also occur.

5. Property: Its Rights and Responsibilities[1]

The land shall not be sold for ever: for the land is mine; for ye are strangers and sojourners with me. (Lev. 25:23)

The private ownership of property is so inextricably mixed up with the market ideology that the rights and obligations of property deserve a full chapter in a discussion of justice in the market economy. Even in a market economy, however, property could in theory be owned by public collectivities, and indeed it sometimes is.

Stewardship

The Christian understanding of property, both Protestant and Catholic, starts from the axiom that God is the owner of everything. He appoints humanity to be his stewards: it is responsible before him for the management of his goods. On the other hand, the steward's duty is to meet the needs of others. The movement from God as owner to the obligation to use one's goods for the benefit of others springs from the double commandment "Thou shalt love the Lord thy God with all thy heart, and with all thy soul, and with all thy strength, and with all thy mind; and thy neighbour as thyself" (Luke 10:27). It is through love of one's neighbour that one expresses, gives body to, one's love of God.

The Bible does not give property a purely individual significance: it has no conception of it other than its objective in service:[1] "What each one had, he did not have for himself to enjoy all alone, taking no account of others..." (Calvin, on Acts 4:32,34). Thomas Aquinas (1225-74) had already said much the same thing.

Furthermore, the service is not only to other individuals, but to the community as such.

> There is no doubt that [God] recommends liberality and all other obligations by which the company and community of humankind are maintained. And therefore, so as not be condemned before God as thieves, we must make as much effort as we can so that what each one possesses he keeps carefully and it procures utility for our sisters and brothers, neither more nor less than for ourselves (Calvin on Ex. 20:15).

Swiss property law reflects this kind of social destination of property: "Property is guaranteed only within the limits drawn by the legal order in the public interest."[2]

Property is not restricted to goods. In the Protestant tradition people own their talents, their ability to render services. Indeed, the word "talent" acquired its present-day meaning by extension from its original meaning as a unit of weight and currency, precisely because of the broader reading that was given to the parable of the talents (Matt. 25:14-30). To say that one owns these capacities is of course to say that we are responsible for putting them at the service of others.

Theft

> [Stealing] is not restricted to money, merchandise or other goods. It is equally theft to deprive a neighbour of a right, whichever it may be. We defraud our neighbour of what belongs to him if we turn away from him the services which we owe him. For he who does not fulfil unto others the duties which his vocation carries, holds back what belongs to them... Theft... is whatever means we use to enrich ourselves at the expense of others.[3]

We are entitled to our share of the fruits provided that others receive theirs. In particular, if we leave to the others a share which amounts to less than they would have had in the absence of the transaction, that constitutes theft. It can be convincingly argued that the essence of any economic transaction is that all parties to it benefit. Much later than the Reformation, economic theory captured this idea through the devices of consumer and producer surplus. In a narrow sense the idea applies to the buyer and the seller, but it should also include those affected by externalities of the transaction.

Priority to the poor

Secondly, the needs of the poor are urgent; they must be met before those of others because the poor cannot wait; Basil, a father of the church (329-379), made the point succinctly: "To the hungry belongs the bread which you keep." Holding something back is the key issue, more than the intent to deprive someone of something permanently, notwithstanding the dictionary definition of "theft" ("theft: dishonest appropriation of another's property with intent to deprive him or her of it permanently", *Concise Oxford English Dictionary*). Of course, simply to hold back from the poor something essential to their very survival amounts from their point of view to depriving them of it permanently.

The "Coase theorem" is particularly apposite where priority to the poor is concerned. Dealing with pollution as an externality, Coase[4] established that whoever – the polluter or the polluted – owns the rights affected by pollution has strictly no influence on the ultimate optimum degree of pollution as established by a pricing system. This has an obvious bearing on income distribution: preference may be given to the poor in allocating the ownership of resources from which a positive income can be derived without altering the efficiency of the outcome.[5] (Ronald Coase was awarded the Nobel prize in economics in 1991.)

To fructify

> In the Protestant ethic, the order of property does not lead to waste, to idleness or to contempt of property.[6]

If everything available to humanity is provided by God with the intention of meeting human needs, it is evident that property must not remain unused. On the contrary it must yield the services which God intends.

> There is nothing more unreasonable than to bury rather than to put to some profitable use the gifts of God, of which the virtue consists properly in bearing fruit. (Calvin on Matt. 25:13)

The parable of the talents – to which the comment just quoted refers – sets the tone in this regard.[7] The stewards who invested the talents with which their master had entrusted them received yet more to manage, but the talent which the unprofitable servant had buried was confiscated (the phrase "unprofitable servant" is in the parable, v.30).

Ownership as a management technique

By distributing the rights and obligations of ownership among a number of proprietors, the social objective can be effectively met. Ownership is a technique for decentralizing decision-making.

The owners are motivated, firstly because they are given responsibility. The Protestant ethic shares the view that without the esteem, including self-esteem, which goes with responsibility, there is less incentive to do a job properly. The owner feels involved with his property; this inspires him to look after something with which he identifies, and the state of which reflects on him. The following passage provides an example:

> Affirming our responsibility as shareholders, we want the Nestlé management to hear arguments inspired by a Christian ethic... Many of us are sentimentally attached to this enterprise, with which our parents and sometimes grandparents were already involved. It is a family affair in a way, and that is why the criticisms expressed [against the company's behaviour] affect us so deeply.[8]

CANES – Convention d'actionnaires Nestlé – was an association of ethically concerned Nestlé shareholders. André Biéler was among its founders. It was succeeded in 2000 by Actares – Actionnaires pour une économie durable. (For more information see www.actares.ch.)

There is, however, a danger of emotional involvement going too far, if the owner becomes so attached to his property that he forgets its social destination. The New Testament warns repeatedly against this danger, e.g., "Lay not up for yourselves treasures upon earth, ...for where your treasure is, there will your heart be also" (Matt. 6:19,21).

Secondly, ownership as a way of assigning management responsibilities has the practical advantage of linking rewards and losses to the owners' effectiveness as managers, thus stimulating their effort and care, and in particular their concern to protect the property in their care: "God does not want things treated like prey, as if they were owned in common, but that everyone own what he has and enjoy it without dispute" (Calvin on Deut. 23:24-24:4). Calvin was already aware of the tragedy of the commons.[9]

MANAGING THE COMMONS

Garrett Hardin's name is associated with the idea that if anyone can have free and uncontrolled access to a common resource, there is a danger that it may be over-exploited, to the detriment of other users present and future. His own formulation was sloppy, arousing the vigorous disapproval of specialists.[10] The underlying idea none the less finds widespread acceptance. Thus *Our Common Future* declares,

> Without agreed, equitable and enforceable rules governing the rights and duties... in respect of global commons, the pressure of demands on finite resources will destroy their ecological integrity over time. Future generations will be impoverished, and the people who suffer most will be those who live in poor countries that can least assert their own claims in a free-for-all.[11]

All agree that some form of social control is indispensable, but Dasgupta underlines the key point for an essay on justice in the market economy:

> I shall not be arguing that wherever feasible common-property resources should cease to remain common property, that private property rights should in such circumstances be encouraged. Market exchanges emanating from the establishment of private-property rights are but one form of social control over resources. They are by no means necessarily the most commendable... [12]

DO SHAREHOLDERS OWN THEIR COMPANY?

If ownership entails the responsibility of management, it makes no sense to say that someone owns something if that person cannot take and implement the decisions which its management entails.

It is generally said that shareholders own their company. The fact that it is repeatedly said is beginning to nudge reality towards its fulfilment, but in fact at present shareholders have virtually no power over how their company is run. In

Swiss law, which is not very different from that of other Western economies, the shareholder has the right to the wealth and income linked to his title, and protective rights intended to protect his position as an investor.[13]

The law requires shareholders to constitute themselves into a general assembly, but in principle it meets only once a year. Thus constituted, they are required to elect a board of directors, and this board has the exclusive responsibility for managing the company. The directors must personally discharge their executive functions; they are inalienable and certainly cannot be delegated to the general assembly of shareholders.

Shareholders have the right to information, but only in so far as it is necessary to the exercise of their rights as shareholders. It is in this perspective that they are required to appoint auditors.

Shareholders can propose resolutions to the general assembly, provided that if they were adopted they would be consistent with the law and the statutes of the company. They cannot therefore intervene in the area which is the inalienable responsibility of the board of directors. Indeed, the responsibility of the directors can be contrasted with the irresponsibility of the shareholders. There is disagreement among lawyers in Switzerland as to whether shareholders have an obligation of loyalty to their company. Loyalty is an integral part of stewardship.

In short, what shareholders own is little more than a financial instrument and some rights to protect its value. Even if some might find it extreme to draw the conclusion that shareholders do not own their company, one can at least confidently conclude that ownership is the sum of a variable set of rights. Rather than argue about the point at which the set becomes so small that to talk of ownership becomes too grand, it may be more helpful to recognize that each particular right associated with the possibility of taking managerial decisions constitutes ownership to that precise extent.

If one takes that position, one must by the same token accept that there can be several owners of a single item of property, each category of owner holding distinct types of power to exercise managerial responsibilities. To take a more down-to-earth example, the owner of a villa owns the right to plant roses in her garden, but the electricity company may own a right to run cables underneath them and indeed to dig the roses up to get at the cables. Nor does the villa-owner necessarily own the right to mow her lawn on Sunday, since her neighbours own an over-riding right to quiet on that day (under present-day Geneva law, in any event).

To keep

The duty of the steward is to keep the property with which he is entrusted. "Keep" has two meanings in this context: to look after and to retain possession.

TO LOOK AFTER

> We own what God has put in our hands on condition that we content ourselves with using it soberly and moderately, keeping what is left over. The owner of a field collects its yearly fruits in such a way that he does not allow the property to decay through neglect, but he takes trouble so that he can pass it on as well cultivated as he received it or better. Calvin's word for "pass it on" is "bailler", which Harraps defines as "to farm out".[14] It is related to "baillif", which in Switzerland can correspond to "steward". He lives from its fruits in such a way that he damages nothing through excess and allows nothing to spoil or perish through neglect... For there to be such diligence to maintain the goods of which God has given us enjoyment, let everyone realize that he is God's steward in everything he owns. (Calvin on Gen. 2:15)

The word Calvin actually uses is *le dépensier*. It is an expressive word, drawing more attention to the act of spending *(la dépense)* than to that of acquiring. It names an office in monastic establishments of which the technical equivalent in English is the now abstruse word "manciple". It is the person entrusted with buying provisions for the community. Thus firstly he is a steward in a spending role and secondly he is at the service of a community.

Calvin insists on the duty to respect the environment. Humanity does not have unlimited rights over nature. Its integrity must be protected. Unnecessary damage must be avoided, and not only when it may correspond to waste in economic terms.

> Here is a general rule of which we should take good note; it is that every time we are tempted to do some damage or harm, let us drive into our memory: our Lord has lodged us in the world, he has given us the things he knew to be useful for our life; now if I want to strip the earth of what God has given it for the nourishment of humanity, ...am I worthy that the earth sustain me ... which is as much for my neighbours as for me? ...There (I say) is what must restrain us should we be tempted by some malice and poisoned to the extent of spoiling trees and houses and similar things. (Calvin on Deut. 20:16-20)

The conjunction of trees and houses is worth noting. On the one hand, the passage of Deuteronomy on which Calvin is commenting explicitly has fruit trees in mind. They are capital goods like houses; they were planted in the same way that houses were built. On the other hand, houses like trees are part of the bounty which is to hand for each generation to enjoy. Humanity is surrounded by the things useful for its life. Whether they were made by humanity is not the important issue. What is important is that in any case they are not to be wantonly spoiled or wasted.

Rest and moderation: the sabbath

The injunction to sobriety and moderation is founded on the institutions of the sabbath and the sabbatical year.

The sabbath requires the master – the owner or manager, the steward in a word – to grant regular rest to those who work for him:

> Six days shalt thou labour, and do all thy work: but the seventh day is the sabbath of the Lord thy God: in it thou shalt not do any work, thou, nor thy son, nor thy daughter, nor thy manservant, nor thy maidservant, nor thine ox, nor thine ass, nor any of thy cattle, nor thy stranger that is within thy gates; that thy manservant and thy maidservant may rest as well as thou. And

remember that thou wast a servant in the land of Egypt and that the Lord thy God brought thee out thence. (Deut. 5:13-15)

Verse 14 recalls Genesis 2:2-3: the creation lasted seven days, and God *rested on the seventh day from all his work*. Rest is an integral part of the creation.

Verse 15 underlines that ceaseless work is a characteristic of slavery. The passage makes two complementary points in this regard: first, the master is not to treat his workers like slaves, milking them to the limit; secondly, the master himself is not to be a slave to production, but to moderate his wants. In present-day terms ox, ass and cattle would count as property, while servants, i.e. workers, would count as stakeholders in the enterprise. In the times the passage was written the distinction was not so clear: the workers may also have been property. It is the owner's responsibility not to treat even his slaves like slaves (cf. Deut. 15:12-14)! In a nutshell, the dignity of freedom includes freedom in relation to the economic imperative. That is a point which the Puritan tradition has tended to forget.

The sabbatical year extends the concept of rest to the land: "But in the seventh year shall be a sabbath of rest unto the land..." The land is not to be cultivated or harvested in that year (Lev. 25:2-5). The land must not be exhausted. This injunction can be extended: no kind of property may be excessively exploited; the capital is not to be run down.[15]

TO RETAIN

God has entrusted property to man as a tool to produce what is needed for himself and all who depend on him, and especially for the poor. The owner should not part from his tool without good reason, for that would amount to shunning his responsibility.[16]

The worker, accustomed to earning his living and feeding his children by his work, would do ill to sell his property unless constrained by necessity. So if we keep what the Lord has put in our hands, provided that while we feed ourselves and our family soberly and honestly we extend a portion to the poor, there is a greater virtue in that than in dissipating and abandoning everything. (Calvin on Matt. 19:29)

The word "abandoning" in this quotation deserves underlining. Calvin is commenting on the passage of Matthew in which Jesus is inviting a rich man to sell what he has, give the proceeds to the poor and follow him; Calvin is urging the reader not to jump hastily to a wrong conclusion about the point of the story. If owning property is wrong, then to sell it to someone else is simply to pass the buck, not to face the essential problem. This approach challenges the attitude so prevalent in the financial market, with its emphasis on liquidity, which is precisely the ability to part at a moment's notice with one's productive assets, to part company with all those who, working with those assets, had made it possible for them all together to produce goods and services.

This is one aspect of the issue of loyalty in taking one's responsibilities on which the Protestant tradition places great weight. Simply to pass a problem on is to show contempt for the property, for those involved in its functioning and for the next owner.

On the other hand, there can be emergency situations in which the question is no longer simply that of sharing out the fruits of productive activity; it may be necessary to break into the capital stock to meet the needs of the poor. "One must meet the needs of the poor, not just... out of what we have to excess, but without even sparing our inheritance if current revenue is insufficient" (Calvin on Matt. 6:19).

This view can be recognized in Rawls's conclusion that inequality is justified to the extent that the poorest are better off as a result of it.[16] In so far as the given ownership of property yields a higher return to the poorest than redistributing it directly to the poor, then it is better to maintain the existing pattern.

FAIR DISTRIBUTION: THE JUBILEE

Notwithstanding the importance of keeping what one owns, the over-riding social objective of ownership sets limits to retention. These are given a temporal dimension in the jubilee message (Lev. 25:8-54 – see chap. 2). Every fifty years the slaves will be freed and the land will be returned to its original owners. The jubilee also involves writing off debts. [In the jubilee]

> the state of the people was renewed with respect to persons, to houses and to the capital represented by fields. By this means God provided for the public needs and supported the poor so that their liberty was not oppressed. (Calvin on Lev. 25:8)

Herein lies part of the meaning of the injunction, "The land shall not be sold for ever: for the land is mine; for you are strangers and sojourners with me" (Lev. 25:23). Even if the owner is managing his property well, the dynamics of the economy, which extend far beyond the reach of any owner, are such that to whomever "that hath shall be given, and he shall have abundance, but from him that hath not shall be taken away even that which he hath" (Matt. 25:29). This structural dynamic calls for a structural response which should not be taken as a reflection on whether or not any individual was behaving properly.

A side effect of assigning ownership to some rather than to others is the concentration not only of wealth but also of power.[17] Power is of course an essential characteristic of property as a management technique. In the Protestant ethic the concentration of both power and wealth are undesirable, since both restrict the area of autonomy or of responsibility open to others. The jubilee stresses the importance of combatting the concentration of either.

Property rights are thus not only conditional on proper management, they take the form of what amounts to a leasehold so that they can be redistributed according to the demands of justice. If the two elements of this pair of conditions are met, the decentralization of property rights can satisfy the requirements of both efficiency and equity.

The ownership of consumer goods

In the Protestant ethic the foregoing set of arguments colours the rights and responsibilities of owning not only producer goods or capital, but also consumer goods.

First, resources which can bear fruit for others should not be distracted from that use. It is part of that argument, and no contradiction with it, to insist that people should own whatever they need to make life easy and convenient for themselves. One's talents, one's time, are part of what one can fructify for the good of society. If by depriving oneself of conveniences one must spend more time and effort coping with one's own affairs, there is that much less which can be devoted to service to others.[18] Conversely, whatever one holds back as private belongings beyond what is needed for convenient living is sterilized, or indeed stolen from the poor. What this adds up to is the sobriety or simplicity which is traditionally regarded as a distinctive mark of the life-style of the Protestant wealthy. It is revealing in this regard to compare 18th century English and American furniture of the same basic styles. The pieces from Puritan America tend to be less ornate, more sober, than those from Anglican Britain.[19]

> While our natural penchants, excited by the stimulations of our consumer society, push us to be spendthrift for ourselves and stingy for others, the liberation which our faith brings leads us on the contrary to be sober for ourselves and generous for others. Not *severe asceticism*, but *joyful sobriety* and *lucid generosity*.[20]

With respect to what one does own as private belongings which cannot be fruitful, the Protestant injunction to look after them still applies. Even these goods are to be held in that sense in a spirit of stewardship.

An operational conclusion

The essential operational conclusions of the approach to property rights described in this chapter hold in a few sentences. First, property rights should be assigned to whomever is best placed to manage the property in the public interest. Secondly, it should not be assumed that it is necessary to assign all the rights over a given item, i.e. managerial responsibilities for it, to a single owner: they can be divided up and allocated in whichever way best meets the first objective. Thirdly, efficiency is not the only goal: over-riding priority is due to the needs of the poor. Finally, and in any event, the allocation of property rights is essentially a matter of public policy.

6. Kinds of Justice

How long will ye judge unjustly, and accept the persons of the wicked? Defend the poor and fatherless: do justice to the afflicted and needy. Deliver the poor and needy: rid them out of the hand of the wicked. (Ps. 82:2-4)

The market performs two distinct functions at once. On the one hand it *allocates* goods and services in response to supply and demand. On the other it *distributes revenue to* the factors of production. These two functions raise – and entangle – the issues of commutative and distributive justice. Divine justice is however prior to both of these.

Divine justice

Divine justice resides in the boundless generosity of God which we cannot begin to repay:

> God is not only just because he gives each person his proper share, in the manner in which people describe justice, because if we wanted to measure it by this yardstick, we would come to think that we were something without him. What is ours? Nothing. Everything is his, what we have and what we are. He is under no obligation to give us what we consider to be ours. In short, nothing is ours and everything he gives belongs to him.[1]

Divine justice sets the stage, or rather the table: it lays out all riches for the enjoyment of humanity. This chapter explores the sharing of these riches. It moves into the domain of human justice, inside economics.

The scholastics essentially relied in their arguments on two types of justice: commutative and distributive. We shall examine them first, but we shall then look at some other forms of justice.

Commutative justice

Commutative justice concerns exchange. Exchange is fair if the items exchanged are of equal value. Roughly speaking, the parties to the transaction should feel that it was fair. Commutative justice involves the golden rule known in a wide range of the world's ethical traditions and stated in Matthew 7:12 as follows:

> All things whatsoever ye would that men should do to you, do
> ye even so to them: for this is the law and the prophets.

Commutative justice rules out the abuses of the market described by chapter 3, in particular cheating and taking advantage of unequal power.

Strictly speaking, commutative justice is restricted to the direct parties to any transaction, the buyer and the seller. It ignores externalities – the consequences of the transaction for third parties. It also ignores the way in which sets of transactions build relationships over time. In this respect, to concentrate on commutative justice strengthens the market ideology, which privileges the transaction to the detriment of the relationship, a choice which can easily undermine the foundations of society.[2]

The ideology of the market rests on an assumption that relations between participants are symmetrical. Commutative justice is an expression of virtue within this assumption. The contract is the epitome of this view. Yet asymmetry is a fundamental element of human relations:

> People seem to forget that the human race could not have sur-
> vived without the gift; that it is more essential than exchange...
> Parents give, children receive. From parents to children there is
> a downward flow of services and goods, without reciprocity.
> What parents do for the child is not in execution of a contract
> agreed with it.[3]

The asymmetrical gift relationship between people should itself be seen in the perspective of divine justice, of the free and boundless gift of the grace of God

Distributive justice

In economics, distributive justice concerns the distribution of revenue, wealth or entitlements between members of society. The market generates a distribution of revenue between factors of production. Since these factors are themselves exchanged on the market, commutative and distributive justice become entwined at this point. It is not so much the market, but a social convention which determines that a doctor earns more than a plumber. This type of attitude is even more taken for granted in a wider geographical perspective: most people consider it normal that a worker in the third world should earn far less than one in a developed country. Few people consider it odd that a peasant in the third world should receive the same income for nurturing a banana over nine months as a shopkeeper in a developed country receives for keeping it in his shop overnight.

Above all, distributive justice raises the question of those who are outside a given transaction, those who are affected by externalities, whether benefits or costs; or those who share in the benefits of collective goods. Distributive justice also concerns those who, having no assets and unable to work, are outside the market: children, the aged, the ill and the handicapped.

Should justice be blindfold?

Justice is traditionally portrayed blindfold. James gives the reasons in compelling words:

> If there come unto your assembly a man with a gold ring, in goodly apparel, and there come in also a poor man in vile raiment; and ye have respect to him that weareth the gay clothing, and say unto him, Sit thou here in a good place; and say to the poor, Stand thou there, or sit here under my footstool: are ye not then partial in yourselves, and are become judges of evil thoughts? Hearken, my beloved brethren, hath not God chosen the poor of this world rich in faith, and heirs of the kingdom which he hath promised to them that love him? But ye have despised the poor. Do not rich men oppress you, and draw you before the judgment seats? Do not they blaspheme that worthy name by the which ye are called? If ye fulfil the royal law according to the scripture, Thou shalt love thy neighbour as thyself, ye do well: but if ye have respect to persons, ye commit sin, and are convicted by the law as transgressors. (2:2-9)

If showing partiality means allowing privileges to the rich and powerful, it is contrary to the "royal law". To pay no regard to social condition is certainly an improvement. On the other hand, as the Bible reminds us again and again, we are expected to go even further and to give priority to the poor. Suffice it to recall what Jesus said at the beginning of his ministry:

> The Spirit of the Lord is upon me, because he hath anointed me to preach the gospel to the poor; he hath sent me to heal the broken hearted, to preach deliverance to the captives, and recovering of sight to the blind, to set at liberty them that are bruised, to preach the jubilee, the acceptable year of the Lord (Luke 4:18-19; "The acceptable year of the Lord" corresponds to the jubilee).

That passage harks back not only to Isaiah 61:1-2, but to the magnificent passage, Isaiah 58:6-9:

> Is not this the fast that I have chosen? To loose the bands of wickedness, to undo the heavy burdens, and to let the oppressed go free, and that ye break every yoke? Is it not to deal thy bread to the hungry, and that thou bring the poor that are cast out to thy house? When thou seest the naked, that thou cover him; and that thou hide not thyself from thine own flesh? Then shall thy light break forth as the morning, and thine health shall spring forth speedily: and thy righteousness shall go before thee; the glory of the Lord shall be thy rearguard. Then shalt thou call, and the Lord shall answer; thou shalt cry, and he shall say, Here I am.

To blindfold justice is progress over kow-towing to privilege, but to remove the blindfold in order to see the poor and the oppressed is even greater progress.

A BLINDFOLD MARKET?

The Quakers, a movement within the radical reformation, are proud of the pioneering role they played in insisting on fixed prices: they charged the same price to everyone regardless of condition. This corresponds in market behaviour to blindfolding justice.

WHO BENEFITS FROM BARGAINING?

At a meeting of the East African Sciences Association in Dar es Salaam in the mid-1960s, a group of expatriate economists were discussing shopping for food in their local markets. One said that his family sent their cook to shop for them. Since white expatriates were obvious to spot and known to be well off, they would be charged higher prices than local people.

Another, who lived in Mauritius, said that they shopped for their servants as well as themselves. Since they were obviously well off, the stallholders knew that they could afford to shop around and indeed to wait for a better opportunity if prices were too high. The needs of a local shopper, who was likely to be poor, were surely urgent. Besides, the servants might be in debt to certain stallholders, which further reduced their bargaining power. The rich shopper would in those circumstances get a lower price.

In the mirage of a market economy that the neo-liberals see, the market is composed of a myriad of buyers and sellers, each singly so insignificant that they cannot influence the overall outcome: that is an essential characteristic of competition as understood in their vision. In the market economy as it really exists, there are some large agents, powerful enough to enjoy latitude in fixing prices; roughly speaking, they can be called monopolies. Monopoly power can take the blindfold off justice. The consequence may lie in the direction of greater justice as we have just described it.

Monopolies can practise discriminatory pricing. By segmenting their market into distinct parts, they can charge a different price in each. An essential requirement of this method is that it not be possible for the different segments to trade with each other in the good or service in question. Otherwise, as in the examples in the box, the agent with access to the lowest price will buy for the others.

On the one hand, a monopoly resorting to discriminatory pricing can charge more to the rich; when that market is saturated, it sets a lower price for a less prosperous segment and so on. In this way it increases its total sales and revenue, and hence increases profit of course. At the same time, however, it makes its product available at a lower price to those who cannot afford to pay a higher one, thus bending over to help the poorer.

On the other hand, discriminatory pricing can be used to opposite effect. Deregulation of the electricity market – one which inevitably has monopolistic features – normally results in lower prices being offered to consumers with countervailing power,[4] i.e. to large customers, while higher prices are charged to small users, who may in certain conditions be poorer.

A further option open to monopolies is to cross-subsidize different segments of their market, even if it is charging a uniform price to everyone. This was until recently common practice among public services like the post or telephones. The standard price of a postage stamp was more than enough to cover the costs of delivering mail in high-density urban conditions; the surplus covered the losses incurred in serving scattered small users. Of course the scattered small users were not always poorer: they included wealthy occupants of remote secondary residences. For these and other reasons, cross-subsidization got a bad name and has gone out of fashion. A more careful examination of who was subsidizing whom could, however, have led to finer tuning to the benefit of the poor.

To sum up all the foregoing arguments, to blindfold justice is rough justice indeed. It is the ostrich's technique for hiding oneself from one's own flesh. One needs to have both eyes wide open to see whether the heavy burdens are undone and the oppressed let free.

Other forms of justice

The list of forms of justice can be indefinitely extended and subdivided: it is open-ended. A few further types of justice can be mentioned with respect to the justice of the market economy. Two of them, *procedural justice* and *restorative justice*, are discussed below. Another type of justice, *retributive justice*, is the subject of chapter 7.

Before moving on to them, it is worth mentioning civic duty, which Catholic moral theology used oddly to call *legal justice*. Commutative and distributive justice concern what accrues to each person. Civic duty completes the set by examining what each person owes to the collectivity as a whole. It includes paying one's taxes, respecting the public domain and taking part in the community's political life at least by voting.[5]

PROCEDURAL JUSTICE

Procedural justice focuses on the social processes which generate outcomes acceptable to all concerned; they can in that regard by and large be called fair. Such justice is more likely to be achieved through processes in which all those concerned can not only take part, but be taken seriously. It involves taking divergent opinions into account with all the weight which the injunction to love one's neighbour as oneself calls into play. Procedural justice occupies a major place in John Rawls's philosophy.[6] It is related to Jürgen Habermas's ethics of discussion,[7] although Habermas does not share Rawls's strong individualism.

> Although very discreet about his confessional origins, Habermas appears as a fairly typical manifestation of the committed Protestant intellectual, careful to defend the democratic foundations of the real world and to protect politics from totalitarian tendencies...[8]

The Polluter-Pays Principle, according to which "the polluter should bear the expenses of carrying out the... measures *decided by public authorities* to ensure that the environment is in an *acceptable state* (emphasis added)", is a case of procedural justice at work (cf. chapter 1). When all is said and done, the people concerned should feel that the state of their environment is acceptable. The process leading to this result is a political one, not a market automatism; the requirement that the measures be decided by public authorities underlines that issue.

We have seen in chapter 2 that the processes of the market left to themselves lead to an inexorable worsening of the condition of the poor and a widening gap between rich and poor. The overall dynamic of the market, as opposed to each transaction taken in isolation, is essentially unjust, in that it leads step by step to unjust results. Only when it is canalized and controlled by processes of another order – normally political ones – can it achieve the objective of providing people with goods and services fairly.

RESTORATIVE JUSTICE

Taken in its general, intuitive sense, restorative justice involves healing a community which has been wounded by an offence. By recalling the essential value of the community and the role of forgiveness in maintaining it, it undermines the market ideology. It constitutes a response to misbehaviour more consonant with the ideals of the New Testament than retributive justice. "Mercy rejoices against judgment" (James 2:13).

Paul expressed misgivings about recourse to the courts:

> If then you have judgments of things pertaining to this life, set them to judge who are least esteemed in the church. I speak to your shame. Is it so, that there is not a wise man among you? No, not one that shall be able to judge between his brethren? But brother goes to law with brother, and that before the unbelievers. Now therefore there is utterly a fault among you, because ye go to law one with another. Why do you not rather take wrong? Why do you not rather suffer yourselves to be defrauded? Nay, you do wrong, and defraud, and that your brethren. (1 Cor. 6:4-8)

This passage makes two points. First, it reproaches the Christians of Corinth for taking their disputes to outsiders for judgment instead of handling them among themselves; in this way it insists on the importance of maintaining the life of the community itself. Secondly, it rails against the very idea of seeking reparation for a wrong – an opinion which James echoes.

The term "restorative justice" has yet another meaning, according to which it refers to a special case of retributive justice (chapter 7): it was appropriated in the Anglo-Saxon culture by a particular technique in which the individual offender and victim confront each other face to face to agree on reparation to the victim by the offender who has been brought to contrition (see www.restorativejustice.org – this site contains a section, called "Chapel" which presents restorative justice in a Judeo-Christian setting.) Restorative justice in this sense springs from the same psychological considerations as the market economy, involving individual transactions between two parties on the one hand (although it does not totally ignore the community as a further stake-holder), and a context in which any taking must be matched by a corresponding giving.

Love for one's neighbour: more élan for divine justice

Over-riding not only the technical characteristics of the just price but also the considerations of commutative and dis-tributive justice is the fundamental imperative of *love for one's neighbour*: "Thou shalt love thy neighbour as thyself" (Matt. 22:39).

That imperative is socially, but not altogether, fundamen-tal. It is a reflection of the other one, "Thou shalt love the Lord thy God with all thy heart, and with all thy soul, and with all thy mind" (Matt. 22:37), which in turn is the least we can do to respond to God's boundless love for us which con-stitutes divine justice. To love one's neighbour as oneself corresponds to the uninterrupted motion of a bouncing ball: God's gifts fall upon us undeservedly and our job is to act in such a way that this bounty passes on to our neighbour, in such a way that our neighbour can in turn pass it on further, and so on.

7. Retribution in a Market Perspective

Retributive justice concerns the codification of revenge. It finds its way into a discussion of justice in the market when penalties for wrongdoing are handled as market transactions. Since the United States frequently resorts to this practice and it is beginning to spread from there to other parts of the world, one cannot avoid examining it here. The tradition has a long history in North America: "Among many Indians of... North America, blood payment was mandatory after killings in order to make peace possible... In most places there was no fixed standard, each group demanding as large an amount as possible".[1]

THE LAW OF THE TALION

"Retaliate" and "talion" both have their root in the same Latin word *talis*, which means "such". The law of the talion (Latin *lex talionis*) was a principle developed in early Babylonian law that criminals should receive as punishment precisely those injuries and damages they had inflicted upon their victims. Many early societies applied this "eye-for-an-eye and tooth-for-a-tooth" principle quite literally. In ancient Babylonian, biblical, Roman and Islamic law, it was a principle operative in private and familial settlements. In early Palestine, injury and bodily mutilation as well as theft were considered private wrongs. It was not for the state to punish the offender; the matter was to be settled between the person who inflicted the injury and the one injured. The same attitude prevailed in early Rome.

The law of the talion was intended to limit retaliation, which always runs the risk of escalation. In the context in which it was developed it was therefore an improvement over unrestrained revenge (Ex. 21:24, Lev. 24:20, Deut. 19:21), but it was still a hard law, as Deuteronomy emphasized in the prefatory phrase "*And thine eye shall not pity*; but life shall go for life, eye for eye, tooth for tooth..."

On the principle that two different persons could not have exactly the same bodily members, the Palestinian sages enacted a law by which the injured party could not demand an eye from the person who caused the loss of his eye but could demand the value of his eye. This led to the abolition of talion in Palestine. In Rome by the 5th century BC, fines had begun to replace talion in many instances.

Even in this modified and less blood-thirsty form, the law of the talion was only a way-station on the journey to the position which Jesus proclaimed in the Sermon on the Mount:

"Ye have heard that it hath been said, An eye for an eye, and a tooth for a tooth: But I say unto you, That ye resist not evil: but whosoever shall smite thee on thy right cheek, turn to him the other also. And if any man will sue thee at the law, and take away thy coat, let him have thy cloak also. And whosoever shall compel thee to go a mile, go with him twain." (Matt. 5:38-41)

(This box is largely based on *Encyclopaedia Britannica* 1999, articles "talion" and "eye for an eye". The references to "Palestinian sages" and "Palestine" are in that source.)

Under the market approach to retributive justice, the wrongdoer pays damages to the victim. The offence has a pair of parties corresponding to a buyer and a seller, and a price can be determined. Justice becomes a private commercial matter. This approach underlies the World Trade Organization's dispute settlement mechanism (see boxes below).

WTO AND THE LAW OF THE TALION

Under the WTO dispute settlement mechanism only the victim of a violation of WTO rules is allowed to take retaliatory measures. WTO attributes vengeance to the victim, ignoring the lessons humanity has learned the hard way over thousands of years and which have led to the conclusion that vengeance belongs to the Lord (Ps. 94:1), or at the very least to society as a whole through its political institutions (Rom. 13). In the WTO case, "society" should be understood as the whole international community.

The weapon is awesome if the victim is powerful, but laughable if the victim is a small country wronged by a great power. It gives a new lease on life to the ancient and barbarous view that might is right.

Part of the progress enshrined in the law of the talion was to confine revenge to the wrongdoer himself, to maintain the cohesion of society by preventing the offence from developing into a feud and spreading. Only the murderer could be murdered in turn.[2] WTO retreats from this early step towards wisdom: the dispute settlement mechanism having recognized one sector of the economy as being the victim of a wrong, the country concerned has the right to choose the sectors of the wrongdoing country on which to retaliate. Thus for instance, in retaliation against the refusal of European consumers to buy hormone beef from the United States, the USA took sanctions against European sheep farmers who produce Roquefort cheese. Similarly, the European Union included citrus fruit in its list of goods to penalize in retaliation against the protectionist duties the United States has imposed on steel. On the other hand, the WTO dispute settlement mechanism meticulously respects the law of the talion in that the value of the retaliatory measures inflicted by the victim on the wrongdoer is not allowed to exceed that of the original damage done.

HOW RETRIBUTION WTO-STYLE WORKS

The original offence
   The trigger is a trade measure which country A takes to protect one of its industries, industry x. The

stakeholders of industry x consider themselves to be the beneficiaries (how the benefits are actually distributed between the different stakeholders is another question). The victims are:

- *the consumers of product x in country A*, since they could have bought the product more cheaply if the industry were not protected;
- *the producers of product x in country B*, who are prevented from exporting to A as much as they might have without the new barriers to entry into country A.

Since these two categories of people are now worse off, they will probably reduce their spending on other products as well; the reduction in prosperity thus spreads further to other sectors of both economies A and B.

Retaliation

Country B challenges A under the WTO dispute settlement mechanism and wins: it is therefore entitled to retaliate against A to an equal amount. It therefore imposes punitive duties on the products of industry y produced in country A. The victims are:

- the producers of product y in country A,
- the consumers of product y in country B,

and, as above, the reduction in prosperity spreads further through both economies.

There are no beneficiaries in this round. As the saying goes, B has cut off its nose to spite its face. Indeed, defenders of pure free trade stress that unilateral trade liberalization benefits the liberalizer, which is true according to the neo-liberal model used in WTO circles of how the economy works. We have seen in chapter 2 that the argument does not hold when unequal parties are concerned in an economic system based on cumulative processes.

> In any event, even under the paw of the talion, the
> original offence is spread through retaliation to new
> and wider circles of victims.

A credible threat of a financial penalty can indeed be effective in influencing the behaviour of profit-oriented entities like enterprises since they are supposed to be guided by financial incentives. The effectiveness of the method is, however, somewhat weakened in so far as the wrongdoer can negotiate the amount to pay. Above all, private economic entities have the choice of escaping the penalty by going bankrupt.

Freedom to negotiate the amount to pay points in the direction of another form of market transaction which is generally considered to fall beyond the outer limits of proper behaviour in the market (chapter 3): blackmail. To defend oneself before the courts or before the WTO dispute settlement mechanism costs something. By merely threatening to engage a procedure of that kind, a party opens the door to an agreement along the lines that an "amicable" settlement can be reached which is cheaper for the party attacked than pursuing the judicial process even if there is strong likelihood of winning it.[3]

Should the victim be paid?

Accepting that exacting a financial penalty from the wrongdoer can be fair and sensible, the question remains whether it should be paid to the victim. It immediately raises another question which recurs throughout the debate on justice in the market economy: Which should be preferred: individual transactions or lasting relationships?[4] If the concern is restricted to the immediate nexus, then there is a strong case for insisting that the offender compensate the victim. If on the other hand the aim is to maintain the cohesion of society as a pleasant environment in which to live, then the overriding objective is to minimize the prospect of the undesirable conduct occurring again. A parallel can be drawn with the Polluter-Pays Principle: the objective is to incite the adoption of control and prevention measures corresponding to the desired social behaviour. These measures may be within the domain of the wrongdoer, the victim, other parties or society as a whole.

However, even if we consider only the wrongdoer and the victim, Ronald Coase showed that in terms strictly of economic efficiency, it makes no difference to the outcome whether the wrongdoer pays the victim or the victim pays the wrongdoer.[5] It follows that the decision on who should meet the costs of the prevention and control measures required depends entirely on considerations of equity, i.e. on which of the parties is best able to carry them.

Even if one accepts that the payment of compensation by the wrongdoer to the victim can be a fair thing to do, there are a number of arguments against such transfers, some resting on grounds of efficiency and others of equity.

The efficiency arguments often fall under the heading of moral hazard. Moral hazard occurs when the prospect of compensation actually encourages prospective beneficiaries to expose themselves to the risk which the policy is intended to avoid. (The award of the 1996 Nobel Prize in economics to James Mirrlees was largely due to his work on moral hazard. However, the bibliography of his works on the Nobel foundation's web site –www.nobel.se/economics/laureates/1996/mirrlees-cv.html – mainly lists unpublished papers on this particular aspect of his work.) As an example, traffic law in Switzerland at least requires that the victim take every possible step to avoid an accident even if he is basically in the right, if he is not to be assigned a share of the blame and the compensation to which he may be entitled be reduced in consequence. Incomplete compensation can encourage people to change their behaviour in a desirable direction. For instance, property owners can thus be encouraged to buy a lock and to lock up their belongings rather than wait for the insurance company to repay them after they are victims of theft.

Who is the victim to be paid?

Who is to be considered the victim to be compensated is not always self-evident. Exodus 21:18-19 describes a clear-cut case:

And if men fight together, and one smite another..., and he die not, but keepeth his bed: if he rise again, and walk abroad upon his staff, then shall he that smote him be quit: only he shall pay for the loss of his time, and shall cause him to be thoroughly healed.

The case in Exodus 21:22 is a bit less straightforward:

If men... hurt a woman with child, so that her fruit depart from her, ... he shall be surely punished, ... and he shall pay as the judges determine.

In the society in which this injunction arose, children contributed sooner or later to the upkeep of the family. The loss of a child was among other things an economic loss which could justify economic compensation. In the same vein, Leviticus 24:18 provided that "he that killeth a beast shall make it good; beast for beast".

In other cases, where the designated beneficiary of the payment in lieu of the direct victim does not directly suffer economic loss, the question of who should receive the payment made by the wrongdoer becomes completely open, the decisive criterion being the one mentioned above: to ensure that prevention and control measures are taken to avoid a repetition of the undesirable behaviour shown in the particular type of case.

Where the payment is not calculated to correspond to the damage done, but set at a higher level – punitive damages – the moral hazard arguments against paying them to the designated victims become even more convincing.

RETRIBUTION AT WORK IN A MARKET FRAMEWORK

Asbestos: Outlandish Claims
More than fifty companies have been driven into bankruptcy since the first asbestos-related law-suit was filed in 1966, in Beaumont, Texas. Many more are likely to go bust.

The [United States] supreme court has twice pleaded with congress to legislate to end the flood of litigation. But the Association of Trial Lawyers, the staunchest opponents of tort reform – that is, reform of personal-injury legislation – is a powerful lobby and has blocked reform measures.

Asbestos litigation in Britain is unlikely ever to reach [US] proportions. Britain's legal system does not impose punitive damages or allow the kind of class-action lawsuits common in [the United States]. The difference between Britain and [the United States], says Robert Mendelsohn, chief executive of Royal & Sun Alliance, Britain's largest non-life insurer, is that in Britain compensation for asbestos is paid to those who are seriously sick, rather than to lawyers and co-claimants in a class-action suit. In [the United States], the dangers are firstly that blanket settlements, meant to resolve all current and future claims, encourage opportunistic claims; and secondly that, as fewer companies have to pay more claims, critically ill victims of asbestos might get inadequate compensation – or none at all.

Quoted from *the Economist*, 25 May 2002 (slightly rearranged).

The social setting

Wrongdoing often springs from a social context in which demanding compensation from the offender in individual cases of transgression (or transactions) is less fair or indeed efficient than changing the context; indeed, the transgressions may in themselves constitute an expression of a desirable social change.

Laws themselves may be illegitimate, a flagrant category being that of laws intended to despoil particular social categories to the benefit of others. The international rules concerning intellectual property rights, peasant communities, indigenous communities and traditional cultures seem to furnish examples of this kind. The rules being developed in the spirit, if not under the *aegis*, of the WTO tend to remove these rights from the communities which developed the intellectual property at stake in order to assign them to enterprises in the transnational economy. When the original communities persist in using them, these enterprises demand the payment of royalties or penalties for illegal use. The common sense of justice would nonetheless lead one to feel that the beneficiaries of such expropriation are hardly entitled to compensation from those they have expropriated. The victory of South Africa against the transnational pharmaceutical companies who wanted to obtain high payments for the use of their patents in treating AIDS is a similar example: the victims – the owners of the patents – were denied compensation from the wrongdoers – those who wanted to breach the then existing international patent rules.

Crime is a particularly common externality which the poor impose on the rich in the cities in the developing world. In the history of Western Europe, far-reaching structural policies involving – inter alia – labour-management relations, education and macro-economic employment policies have greatly reduced personal insecurity compared with a few centuries ago.

On the occasion of an outbreak of pillaging supermarkets by the hungry in Brazil a few years ago, the Roman Catholic Church came out explicitly to remind the public that the poor have the right to satisfy their immediate needs by the means available to them.

Alternatively, the powerful and possessing classes can strengthen the apparatus of repression and exclusion in such way that the poor turn on each other rather than on the rich. The Watts riots of the 1960s are an example which many still remember: provoked by long-standing social injustices, thousands of African-Americans rioted, burned stores, and pillaged the Watts district of Los Angeles in the United States,[6] picking especially on the property of local Asian-Americans. While this method of maintaining the privileges of the wealthy may be economically efficient, it runs against deep-seated notions of justice.[7]

The dynamics of retribution

We have seen that each transaction in the market fits into a context, a relationship, and it participates in the evolution of the relationship. Left to its own devices, the evolution will be in a cumulative direction: whichever the direction of the initial impulse, it will tend to continue in that direction and at an accelerating rate (cf. chapter 2). Retribution follows the same kind of dynamic.

Indeed the way of handling retribution changes through the Bible. It starts in Genesis with punitive damages:

> And the LORD said... "whosoever slayeth Cain, vengeance shall be taken on him sevenfold" ... And Lamech said unto his wives, ... I have slain a man to my wounding, and a young man to my hurt. If Cain shall be avenged sevenfold, truly Lamech seventy and sevenfold". (Gen 4:15, 23-24)

Given the consequences of this sort of retributive inflation, which could be terrible, Israel adopted the law of the talion, which lays down that the measure of retaliation must correspond exactly to the original damage done: "Thou shalt give life for life, eye for eye, tooth for tooth, hand for hand, foot for foot, burning for burning, wound for wound, stripe for stripe" (Ex. 21:23-25).

This approach still has shortcomings. It leads in principle to an unending cycle of repeated violence even if it does not escalate, as the victim of revenge takes revenge in turn.[8]

The New Testament therefore took the radical step of urging that the process needs to be defused so as to bring it to an end. Matthew 18:21-22 clearly recalls the passage in Genesis just quoted:

> Then came Peter to him, and said, Lord, how often shall my brother sin against me, and I forgive him? till seven times? Jesus saith unto him, I say not unto thee, Until seven times: but, Until seventy times seven.

The argument is more fully developed a few verses further in Matthew:

> Ye have heard that it hath been said, an eye for an eye, and a tooth for a tooth: but I say unto you, That ye resist not evil: but whosoever shall smite thee on thy right cheek, turn to him the other also. And if any man will sue thee at the law, and take

away thy coat, let him have thy cloak also. And whosoever shall compel thee to go a mile, go with him two. (5:38-41)

The analysis of the dynamic underlying those sentences stands out in verses 43-44:

Ye have heard that it hath been said, Thou shalt love thy neighbour, and hate thine enemy. But I say unto you, Love your enemies, bless them that curse you, do good to them that hate you, and pray for them which spitefully use you and persecute you.

It is by responding to one's enemy with love that one breaks the cycle of retribution and hatred. The market logic of the law of the talion is overtaken by a more far-sighted view of how people respond, the aim being to build a society which holds together.

CRIME AND PUNISHMENT

Dostoïevsky and Protestant thought

In *Crime and Punishment* and his later novels, Dostoïevsky strives, starting from the Orthodox tradition, to show that the human beings who allow themselves to be invaded by the love of God manage to liberate themselves from the infernal cycle of hatred and violence. Crime and expiation are the immanent law of a humanity which refuses the law of love proposed by a loving God... We discover a God who is suffering because of the sin of the world and who invites us to enter into his suffering. Protestant thought since the mid-20th century (Bonhoeffer, Jüngel, Moltmann, echoing themes of the young Barth) has inherited Dostoïevsky's work.[9]

8. The Just Price

Everyone understands intuitively what a just price is. Everyone feels that some prices are fair while others are not. Yet the just price is one of those economic concepts which fall apart when one tries to get a grip on them. Immensely resilient, deeply rooted in every society where exchange takes place – i.e. in every society – the just price refuses to be forced into any formal analytical or legal mould.

An episode in history

Historically, the high point of the just price as a doctrine lies in the 13th and 14th centuries. In the Christian tradition, the central figure behind it was Thomas Aquinas (1225-74).[1] He of course referred back to Aristotle's *Nicomachean Ethics*, but similar ideas were circulating in the Islamic thought of his own time.[2]

The just price was regarded as a matter of commutative justice. In this perspective it can be seen as an application to the market of the golden rule, "Therefore all things whatsoever ye would that men should do to you, do ye even so to them" (Matt. 7:12). However, once the question of the just price of labour is raised, considerations of distributive justice become inescapable: it is to a decisive extent through wages and salaries that income is distributed through society. Furthermore, the level of income is related to social status. Another scholastic thinker, Duns Scotus (1265-1308), argues explicitly that a just price is one which enables a merchant to support his family adequately. Social status is in turn related to power and influence.

The just price as a tag

Consideration of the just price took a wrong turning when it took to trying to determine which price *tag* to place on a traded good or service. It then headed towards one of two solutions. The first was that the price should correspond to what is considered normal in that particular market. Thus the distribution of income current in the economy becomes a basis for assessing what the just price should be, rather than the object of critical examination in the light of considerations of justice. Consider the senior figures who walk away with millions in their pockets from the ruins of the companies which have collapsed under their command, to the great loss of the workers now without work and sometimes of the taxpayers who must come to the rescue. According to this kind of approach, the executives' remuneration, being normal, is just; indeed, the more widespread this behaviour, the more it is evidently just. Yet this flies in the face of normal feelings of justice. The second was to reduce the just price simply to the price generated by supply and demand. This was the route followed in particular by the Salamanca school in the 16th century, especially Luis Molina.[3] This however begs the whole question of justice.

Both of the above outcomes are essentially conservative, not simply accepting but supporting the status quo. In common thinking, on the other hand, the just price comes to mind precisely when there seems to be something unacceptable about the status quo. The idea of fairness or justice contains some expectations about the quality of relations between the parties involved.

The just price as an approach

Free and equal parties

Within the realm of commutative justice, for a price to be just it must be the outcome of relations between parties who are free and equal. Each of these words is in turn at least as laden with significance and undertones as "the just price" itself.

In any event and limiting ourselves to a model where there are no externalities, these conditions may be achieved in a free market if both the buyer and the seller are in a position where they can decline to conclude the transaction. This implies that either party can turn to another seller or buyer if a more favourable price may be obtained that way, and furthermore that the item in question is not indispensable, so that both parties may refrain from trading, at least for the time being. In short, one can be sure that a free market will generate fair prices only if the items traded are not urgent essentials (which is not to deny that under certain conditions a free market may generate fair prices for such goods as well).

The number of parties

The standard image of the conditions in which a just price is set assumes that only two parties are involved: a buyer and a seller. The number is normally greater, however. If we consider a product sold by or to a large firm, the parties affected by the price – the stakeholders – include the consumers, the firm's employees, its suppliers, those who provided its capital either as lenders or as shareholders, the collectivity – which can be understood to include the environment – and the public authorities. Neo-liberal thought argues that the interests of all these may be adequately met by a set of pair-wise transactions, but there have been enough cases recently to convince the public that it is not automatically so.

Mass dismissals to increase the remuneration of share-holders shock public feelings of justice. They are similarly shocked when fat cats abandon the company they led while the providers of capital they leave behind suffer huge losses, including workers who had invested their savings in company shares, and even more so when taxpayers are called willy-nilly to the rescue.

The debate on tax havens enters into this same category. Tax havens attract taxable activities away from collectivities which need the revenue to cover the costs of the services their members expect of them. Tax competition, forcing revenue down, benefits the inhabitants of low-tax areas to the detriment of those who live in places where the authorities are expected to provide a more costly range of services.[4]

In all the above cases it is not clear whether the matter is one of commutative or distributive justice.

The collectivity may have to bear external costs. The Polluter-Pays Principle has been developed to deal with such situations: the price which meets the principle, ensuring that the environment is in an acceptable state, is the outcome of a political process of negotiation between the various parties involved. This is no more than a modern expression of a traditional manner of determining a just price. On the same Sunday in 1536 on which the people of Geneva voted to adopt the Reformation, it also voted on the price of bread.

A similar arrangement can be found in the Islamic tradition of the just price: Ibn Taimīyah explains a method proposed by one of his predecessors, Ibn Habib. According to him,

> the authority in charge should call a meeting of market representatives. Others also should be admitted to the meeting so that they could verify their statement. After negotiation and investigation about their sale and purchase he should persuade them to a price that can support them as well as the common people. Thus they all might agree.[5]

The solitary Robinson Crusoe is dear to neo-liberal economists in explaining how an economy works. However, as André Biéler points out, there is no model resembling Robinson Crusoe anywhere in the Bible. On the contrary, from the very moment of the creation of Adam "the LORD God said, It is not good that the man should be alone" (Gen. 2:18) and he created Eve.

Exchange is one of the bonds which hold society together. As Calvin says,

> People are born one for the others, and consequently they must communicate among themselves to maintain the human community. Of those who make good use of the gifts they have received from God, it is said that they are trading... because they must exchange and trade one with another in order to maintain the community. Indeed, the industry with which everyone does his work, his very vocation, his dexterity and other gifts are like merchandise because the end and use are that there should be natural communication between people. (on Matt. 25:15,20)

Unjust prices tear the community apart. If people think that they are not fairly treated in trade, they will become alienated from the community and see no reason to sustain it.

J.M. Keynes, undoubtedly the greatest economist of the 20th century, captured this point when he spoke of fair profits:

> The economic doctrine of normal profits, vaguely apprehended by everyone, is a necessary condition for the justification of capitalism. The businessman is only tolerable so long as his gains can be held to bear some relation to what, roughly and in some sense, his activities have contributed to society.[6]

The concept of a just price includes the means of ensuring that all those concerned feel that it is fair. Just prices are the ones with which people feel comfortable; they are not necessarily the ones which correspond to some formula.

> Just measure does not lie, for a Christian, in a rule or norm dictated from outside or coming from some general morals; it is given by the relationship of love which the living Christ establishes between people.[7]

"If you are led by the Spirit, ye are not under the law... For all the law is fulfilled in one word: Thou shalt love thy neighbour as thyself" (Gal. 5:18,14).

Conclusion

To sum up, one could say that an ethical approach to the market involves firstly setting outer limits to the area it should be allowed to cover, secondly striving for conditions of fairness in its inner workings, and above all ensuring that every decision is illuminated by love for one's neighbour.

The market alone cannot attain the ultimate objective of the economy which is the common good. It is rather like a nuclear reactor: although the energy it produces is desirable, it is intrinsically unsafe; it needs to be carefully confined.

The workings of the market produce particular results. They may be efficient; they may even be fair, but regardless of that the love of one's neighbour has something further to contribute. There are many economic problems which we feel in our guts are important, but which the intellectual discipline of economics cannot handle because it lacks the tools it needs. Economists become impatient with notions like speculation, exploitation or just price because they cannot define them with the tools at their disposal. And yet people feel that these concepts are important. Ethics can handle them because that discipline contains in its toolbox the essential element: love of one's neighbour. Speculation, exploitation, unfair prices all involve a failure of love.

Economists like to categorize shortcomings in the workings of the economy as market failures or policy failures. A market failure occurs when the market fails to behave in the way the textbooks say it should; a policy failure occurs when political measures are taken which prevent the market from working in the way the textbooks say it should. Less dogmatic – or more pragmatic – economists might say that market failures occur when the market left to itself fails to achieve the social objectives assigned to it, while policy failures occur when the policies that the political authorities apply lead to inefficient or unintended results.

More fundamental than either of these failures, however, are failures of love. A market, a policy, indeed any action, which fails to express love for one's neighbour as for oneself is a failure in its essence.

Though I speak with the tongues of men and of angels, and have not love, I am become as sounding brass, or a tinkling cymbal. And though I have the gift of prophecy, and understand all mysteries, and all knowledge; and though I have all faith, so that I could remove mountains, and have not love, I am nothing. And though I bestow all my goods to feed the poor, and though I give my body to be burned, and have not love, it profiteth me nothing. Love... rejoiceth not in iniquity, but rejoiceth in the truth (1 Cor. 13:1-3,6).

Notes

Chapter 1

[1] Mudry, Yvan (2003), *Adieu l' économie*, Geneva, Labor et Fides, p.64.
[2] Dommen, Edward (1997), "Paradigms of Governance and Exclusion", *Journal of Modern African Studies*, vol. 35, no. 3, pp.488-90.
[3] Calvin, Jean, Sermon 53, on 1 Tim. 6:17-19. The quotations from Calvin are as a rule drawn from the forthcoming English translation of André Biéler's *La pensée économique et sociale de Calvin*, Geneva, Georg (1961).
[4] Dommen, Edward (1974), *Estimating Non-monetary Economic Activities*, UNDAT, Suva.
[5] World Commission on Environment and Development (1987), *Our Common Future*, Oxford & New York, OUP, p.43.
[6] *Encyclopaedia Britannica*, CD 1999 standard edition, various articles.
[7] Popper, Karl (1959), *The Logic of Scientific Discovery*, London, Hutchinson.
[8] Comeliau, Christian (2000), *Les impasses de la modernité: critique de la marchandisation du monde*, Paris, Seuil, p.67.
[9] OECD (Organisation for Economic Cooperation and Development) (1972), "The Polluter-Pays Principle: Definitions and Recommendations", recommendation of the council on guiding principles concerning international economic aspects of environmental policies (adopted by the council at its 293rd meeting on 26 May 1972); Dommen (1993), *Fair Principles for Sustainable Development*, Aldershot, Edward Elgar.
[10] OECD, "The Polluter-Pays Principle", annex 1.
[11] Baudot, Jacques ed. (2000), *Building a World Community: Globalisation and the Common Good*, Copenhagen, Royal Danish Ministry of Foreign Affairs, pp.46-47.
[12] Note to Matt. 22:39 in the *Traduction œcuménique de la Bible*.

Chapter 2

[1] *Encylopédie Hachette Multimédia*, 99.
[2] Walras, Léon (1874-1877), *Éléments d' économie pure*, (1898), *Études d' économie politique appliquée*, (Walras 1874-1877; 1898).
[3] *Encyclopédie Hachette Multimédia*, 99.
[4] Kissling, Christian ed. (1997), *Quel avenir pour l'État social?* Geneva, Labor et Fides, p.31.
[5] Girard, René (1978), *Des choses cachées depuis la fondation du monde*, Paris, Grasset; English version (1987): *Things Hidden since the Foundation of the World*, Stanford, Stanford UP. (1982), *Le bouc émissaire*, Paris, Grasset; English version (1986): *The Scapegoat*, Baltimore, Johns Hopkins UP. (1986), *La route antique des hommes pervers*, Paris, Grasset.
[6] Dumouchel, Paul, and Jean-Pierre Dupuy (1979), *L'enfer des choses: René Girard et la logique de l'économie*, Paris, Seuil. Herren, André (1989), *Violence et victime: la révélation évangélique dévoile la*

94

violence camouflée et les (en)jeux du désir: un regard sur la violence: l'anthropologie de René Girard, Geneva, Atelier oecuménique de théologie, 3 April (mimeo).

[7] Blaug, Mark (1962), *Economic Theory in Retrospect*, London, Heinemann, p.5.

[8] Dommen (1997), *Quaker Simplicity*, Sunderland, Univ. of Sunderland, p.18.

[9] Dommen (1999), "Heureux anniversaire Sisyphe! Une analyse économique du mythe du jubilé", in *Dette et Jubilé*, Jean-Michel Bonvin ed., Geneva, Observatoire de la Finance.

[10] Trocmé, André (1961), *Jésus-Christ et la révolution non-violente*, Geneva, Labor et Fides, p.31.

[11] *Ibid.*, pp.26-29.

[12] Solomon, Norman (1997), "Economics of the jubilee", in Ucko, Hans (1997), *The Jubilee Challenge: Utopia or Possibility?*, Geneva, WCC, pp.151-52.

[13] Raiser, Konrad (1997), "Utopia and responsibility", in Ucko, *The Jubilee Challenge*, p.23.

[14] Pontifical Council for Justice and Peace (1997), *Towards a Better Distribution of Land*, Vatican, Libreria Editrice Vaticana, §36,8.

[15] Dommen (2000), *Laisser des grapilles: contre la convoitise, la fête*, Lausanne, Pain pour le prochain, collection "Repères" 4/00.

Chapter 3

[1] Zwingli, Huldrych (1522), *Eine göttliche Vermahnung an die ältesten Eidgenossen zu Schwyz.* (1524) *Eine treue und ernstliche Vermahnung an die frommen Eidgenossen.*

[2] *L'Hebdo*, 30 May 2002, Lausanne.

[3] Tuke, James Hack (1882), "Ought Emigration from Ireland to Be Assisted?", *Contemporary Review*, April.

[4] Amin, Samir (1990), *Eurocentrism*, London, Zed, pp.112-13.

[5] Bertrand, Agnès and Laurence Kalafatides (2002), *OMC, le pouvoir invisible*, Paris, Fayard, p.230.

[6] UNESCO (2003), http://www.unesco.org/culture/industries/trade/html_eng/question13.shtml#13, consulted on 29. Sept. 2003.

[7] UNESCO (2003), http://www.unesco.org/culture/industries/trade/html_eng/question16.shtml, consulted on 29. Sept. 2003.

[8] European Union (2001), "Livre blanc sur la gouvernance européenne: Rapport du groupe de travail 3b, Décentralisation. Meilleure implication des acteurs nationaux, régionaux et locaux" (SG-2001-08586-00-00-FR-TRA-00 (EN)).

[9] World Council of Churches (1992), *Christian Faith and the World Economy Today,* a study document, p.36.

[10] Zwingli (1523), *Von göttlicher und menschlicher Gerechtigkeit*, in *Corpus Reformatorum*, vol. 89 (Zwingli Opera Vol.II), p.512.

[11] *Ibid.*

[12]London Yearly Meeting of the Religious Society of Friends, *Christian Faith and Practice in the Experience of the Society of Friends*, London, 1960, §567.

Chapter 4
[1]Schmidheiny, Stephan (1992), "A Global Business Perspective on Development and the Environment", in *Changing Course*, Cambridge MA, MIT Press.
[2]Smith, Adam (1776), *An Inquiry into the Nature and Causes of the Wealth of Nations*, book 4, chapter 2.
[3]Schmidheiny, "A Global", p.29.
[4]Galbraith, J.K. (1971), *The New Industrial State*, 2nd ed. rev., Boston, Houghton Mifflin.
[5]Rawls, John (1971), *A Theory of Justice*, Oxford, OUP.

Chapter 5
[1]An earlier version of this chapter was published as "Property and the Protestant Ethic" in *Metanoia*, vol. 9, no. 4, winter 1999-2000.
[2]Biéler (1961), p.353.
[3]Tanquerel, Thierry, 1994, "Que reste-t-il de la garantie de la propriété?", in Fuchs, Eric and Ossipow, William (1994), *L'homme respecté*, Geneva, Labor et Fides, p.140.
[4]Calvin, Jean, *Institution*, vol.2, chapter 8, §45.
[5]Coase, R.H. (1960), "The problem of social cost", *Journal of Law and Economics*, 3, pp.1-44.
[6]Dommen (1993), *Fair Principles for Sustainable Development*, pp.27-28. Bonus, Holger (1993), "Implications of the Polluter-Pays and the User-Pays Principles for Developing Countries", in Dommen (1993).
[7]Biéler (1961), p.356.
[8]Fuchs, Eric (1999), *Tout est donné, tout est à faire*, Geneva, Labor et Fides, p.47.
[9]CANES (1996), *Historique et présentation*, Trélex, Switzerland, Convention d'actionnaires Nestlé, p.2.
[10]Hardin, G. (1968), "The Tragedy of the Commons", *Science*, p.162.
[11]Dasgupta, Partha (1982), *The Control of Resources*, Oxford, Basil Blackwell, p.13. Lawrence, Roderick (2000), *Property, Rights and Fairness*, Cambridge, EVE Policy Research Brief Series no. 6, p.8.
[12]World Commission on Environment and Development (1987), *Our Common Future*, Oxford & New York, Oxford UP, p.261.
[13]Dasgupta, *The Control of Resources*, p.2.
[14]This section rests largely on Schneider, Jacques-André (1998), "Le droit de l'actionnaire de proposer une résolution au vote de l'Assemblée générale", *Pratique juridique actuelle* (PJA 5/98).
[15]Harraps (1988), *New Standard French and English Dictionary*, London.

96

[16] Biéler (1961), p.356.
[17] *Ibid.*, p.357.
[18] Rawls, *A Theory of Justice.*
[19] Tanquerel, "Que reste-t-il de la garantie de la propriété?", p.194.
[20] Dommen, *Quaker Simplicity.*
[21] Hinckley, F. Lewis (1953), *A Directory of Antique Furniture*, New York, Crown.
[22] Action de Carême/Pain pour le prochain (1984), *Réhabiliter l'argent*, Lausanne, concluding paragraph. Although the booklet under reference is anonymous, André Biéler seems to have played a major role in drafting it. The emphasized words are emphasized in the original.

Chapter 6
[1] Zwingli (1523), *Von göttlicher und menschlicher Gerechtigkeit*, p.475.
[2] Soros, George (1998), *The Crisis of Global Capitalism (Open Society Endangered)*, New York, Public Affairs, esp. chapter 4.
[3] Jouvenel, Bertrand de (1963), *The Pure Theory of Politics*, New Haven, Yale UP.
[4] Galbraith, John Kenneth (1951), *American Capitalism: The Concept of Countervailing Power.*
[5] Perrot, Étienne (2003), "Développement durable: mythe et réalité", *Foi et développement*, no. 316, septembre.
[6] Rawls, *A Theory of Justice.*
[7] Habermas, Jürgen (1981), *Theorie des Kommunikativen Handels*, Frankfurt/Main, Suhrkamp. (1992), *Faktizität und Geltung. Beiträge zur Diskurstheorie des Rechts und des demokratischen Rechtsstaats*, Frankfurt/Main, Suhrkamp.
[8] Müller, Denis (1995), article "Jürgen Habermas", in *Encyclopédie du protestantisme*, Geneva, Labor et Fides/Paris, Cerf.

Chapter 7
[1] *Encyclopedia Britannica* 1999, article "Blood money".
[2] Gillièron, Bernard (1998), *Dictionnaire biblique*, Poliez-le-Grand, Switzerland, Éditions du Moulin, 3rd ed., article "venger".
[3] The foregoing arguments can be found in Jawara, Fatoumata and Aileen Kwa (2003), *Behind the Scenes at the WTO*, London, Zed, in association with Focus on the Global South, Bangkok, pp.6-7.
[4] Soros (1998), *The Crisis of Global Capitalism*, p.73.
[5] Coase, "The Problem of Social Cost".
[6] *Encyclopaedia Britannica*, CD 1999 standard edition.
[7] Dommen, *Fair Principles for Sustainable Development*, p.19.
[8] Kadare, Ismail (1980), *Prilli I thyer*, Tirana (*Broken April*, London & New York 1990). (This theme is depicted in Ismail Kadare's novel *Broken April* [Kadare 1980]; it has twice been made into a film, the more recent one being *Behind the Sun*, by Walter Salles, Brazil 2002).
[9] Gabus, Jean-Paul (1995), article "Châtiment" in *Encyclopédie du protestantisme*.

Chapter 8

[1] Thomas Aquinas (1272), *Summa theologica* (or *Summa theologiae*), especially IIa/IIae question 77.

[2] Islahi, Abdul Azim (1988), *Economic Concepts of Ibn Taimiyah*, Leicester, Islamic Foundation, p.78.

[3] Michel, Christian, (n.d.) *Qu'est-ce que le "juste prix"?*, www.prolib-ertate.org/economie/juste-prix.htm.

[4] Dommen (2002), "Pourquoi faut-il payer les impôts?" in Froidevaux, Dominique, *La Suisse dans la constellation des paradis fiscaux*, Geneva, Editions d'En-bas.

[5] Islahi, *Economic Concepts of Ibn Taimiyah*, p.100.

[6] Keynes, John Maynard (1923), *A Tract on Monetary Reform*.

[7] Biéler (1961), p.452.

Bibliography

Action de Carême/Pain pour le prochain (1984), *Réhabiliter l'argent*, Lausanne

Amin, Samir (1990), *Eurocentrism*, London, Zed

Aristotle, *Nicomachean Ethics*

Baudot, Jacques ed. (2000), *Building a World Community: Globalisation and the Common Good*, Copenhagen, Royal Danish Ministry of Foreign Affairs

Bertrand, Agnès and Laurence Kalafatides (2002), *OMC, le pouvoir invisible*, Paris, Fayard

Biéler, André (1961), *La pensée économique et sociale de Calvin*, Geneva, Georg, English translation forthcoming

Blaug, Mark (1962) *Economic Theory in Retrospect*, London, Heinemann

Bonus, Holger (1993), "Implications of the Polluter-Pays and the User-Pays Principles for Developing Countries", in Dommen 1993

Calvin, Jean: the quotations from Calvin are as a rule drawn from the forthcoming English translation of Biéler 1961

CANES (1996), *Historique et présentation*, Trélex, Switzerland

Coase, R.H. (1960), "The Problem of Social Cost", *Journal of Law and Economics*, 3, pp.1-44

Comeliau, Christian (2000), *Les impasses de la modernité: critique de la marchandisation du monde*, Paris, Seuil

Dasgupta, Partha (1982), *The Control of Resources*, Oxford, Blackwell

Dommen, Edward (1974), *Estimating Non-monetary Economic Activities*, UNDAT, Suva

Dommen, Edward (1993), *Fair Principles for Sustainable Development*, Aldershot, UK, Edward Elgar

Dommen, Edward (1997), *Quaker Simplicity*, Sunderland, UK, Univ. of Sunderland

Dommen, Edward (1997), "Paradigms of Governance and Exclusion", *Journal of Modern African Studies*, 35, 3

Dommen, Edward (1999), "Heureux anniversaire Sisyphe! Une analyse économique du mythe du jubilé", in *Dette et Jubilé*, ed. Jean-Michel Bonvin, Geneva, Observatoire de la finance

Dommen, Edward (2000), *Laisser des grapilles: contre la convoitise, la fête*, Lausanne, Pain pour le prochain, collection "Repères" 4/00

Dommen, Edward (2002), "Pourquoi faut-il payer les impôts?" in Froidevaux 2002

Dumouchel, Paul and Jean-Pierre Dupuy (1979), *L'enfer des choses: René Girard et la logique de l'économie*, Paris, Seuil

Encyclopaedia Britannica CD 1999 standard ed.

Encyclopédie du protestantisme, 1995, Paris, Cerf/Geneva, Labor et Fides

Encyclopédie Hachette Multimédia 99

European Union (2001), *Livre blanc sur la gouvernance européenne: Rapport du groupe de travail 3b, Décentralisation. Meilleure implication des acteurs nationaux, régionaux et locaux* (SG-2001-08586-00-00-FR-TRA-00 (EN))

Froidevaux, Dominique (2002), *La Suisse dans la constellation des paradis fiscaux*, Genève, Editions d'En-bas

Fuchs, Eric (1999), *Tout est donné, tout est à faire*, Geneva, Labor et Fides

Fuchs, Eric and William Ossipow (1994), *L'Homme respecté*, Geneva, Labor et Fides

Gabus, Jean-Paul (1995), article "Châtiment", in *Encyclopédie du protestantisme*

Galbraith, John Kenneth (1951), *American Capitalism: The Concept of Countervailing Power*

Galbraith, John Kenneth (1971), *The New Industrial State*, 2nd ed. rev., Boston, Houghton Mifflin

Gillièron, Bernard (1998), *Dictionnaire biblique*, Poliez-le-Grand, Switzerland, Editions du Moulin, 3rd ed.

Girard, René (1978), *Des choses cachées depuis la fondation du monde*, Paris, Grasset; English version (1987): *Things Hidden since the Foundation of the World*, Stanford, Stanford UP

Girard, René (1982), *Le bouc émissaire*, Paris, Grasset; English version (1986): *The Scapegoat*, Baltimore, Johns Hopkins UP

Girard, René (1986), *La route antique des hommes pervers*, Paris, Grasset

Habermas, Jürgen (1981), *Theorie des Kommunikativen Handels*, Frankfurt/Main, Suhrkamp

Habermas, Jürgen (1992), *Faktizität und Geltung. Beiträge zur Diskurstheorie des Rechts und des demokratischen Rechtsstaats*, Frankfurt/Main, Suhrkamp

Hardin, G. (1968), "The Tragedy of the Commons", *Science*, 162

Harraps (1988), *New Standard French and English Dictionary*, London

Herren, André (1989), *Violence et victime: la révélation évangélique dévoile la violence camouflée et les (en)jeux du désir: un regard sur la violence: l'anthropologie de René Girard*, Geneva, Atelier œcuménique de théologie, 3 April (mimeo)

Hinckley, F. Lewis (1953), *A Directory of Antique Furniture*, New York, Crown

Islahi, Abdul Azim (1988), *Economic Concepts of Ibn Taimiyah*, Leicester, Islamic Foundation

Jawara, Fatoumata and Aileen Kwa (2003), *Behind the Scenes at the WTO*, London, Zed in association with Focus on the Global South, Bangkok

Jouvenel, Bertrand de (1963), *The Pure Theory of Politics,* New Haven, Yale UP

Kadare, Ismail (1980), *Prilli I thyer*, Tirana (*Broken April*, London & New York 1990)

Keynes, John Maynard (1923), *A Tract on Monetary Reform*

Kissling, Christian ed. (1997), *Quel avenir pour l'Etat social?*, Geneva, Labor et Fides

L'Hebdo, 30 May 2002, Lausanne

Lawrence, Roderick (2000), *Property, Rights and Fairness*, Cambridge, EVE Policy Research Brief Series no. 6

London Yearly Meeting of the Religious Society of Friends, *Christian Faith and Practice in the Experience of the Society of Friends*, London, 1960

Mauss, Marcel (1924), *Essai sur le don*

Michel, Christian (n.d.), *Qu'est-ce que le "juste prix"?*, www.pro-libertate.org/economie/juste-prix.htm

Mudry, Yvan (2003), *Adieu l'économie*, Geneva, Labor et Fides

Müller, Denis (1995), article "Jürgen Habermas", in *Encyclopédie du protestantisme*

OECD (Organisation for Economic Cooperation and Development) (1972), "The Polluter-Pays Principle: Definitions and Recommendations", recommendation of the Council on guiding principles concerning international economic aspects of environmental policies (adopted by the Council at its 293rd meeting on 26 May 1972)

Perrot, Étienne (2003), "Développement durable: mythe et réalité", *Foi et développement*, 316, Sept.

Popper, Karl (1959), *The Logic of Scientific Discovery*, London, Hutchinson

Raiser, Konrad (1997), "Utopia and Responsibility", in Ucko 1997

Rawls, John (1971) *A Theory of Justice*, Oxford, Oxford UP

Rousseau, Jean-Jacques (1762), *The Social Contract*

Schmidheiny, Stephan (1992), "A Global Business Perspective on Development and the Environment", in *Changing Course*, Cambridge MA, MIT Press

Smith, Adam (1776), *An Inquiry into the Nature and Causes of the Wealth of Nations*

Schneider, Jacques-André (1998), "Le droit de l'actionnaire de proposer une résolution au vote de l'Assemblée générale", *Pratique juridique actuelle*, 5, 98

Solomon, Norman (1997), "Economics of the Jubilee", in Ucko 1997

Soros, George (1998), *The Crisis of Global Capitalism (Open Society Endangered)*, New York, Public Affairs

Tanquerel, Thierry (1994), "Que reste-t-il de la garantie de la propriété?", in Fuchs and Ossipow 1994

Thomas Aquinas (1272), *Summa theologica* (or *Summa theologiæ*) *Traduction œcuménique de la bible*, Paris, Cerf, 1972

Trocmé, André (1961), *Jésus-Christ et la révolution non-violente*, Geneva, Labor et Fides

Tuke, James Hack (1882), "Ought Emigration from Ireland to be Assisted?", *Contemporary Review*, April

Ucko, Hans (1997), *The Jubilee Challenge: Utopia or Possibility?*, Geneva, WCC Publications

UNESCO (2003a), http://www.unesco.org/culture/industries/trade/html_eng/question13.shtml#13, consulted on 29 Sept. 2003

UNESCO (2003b), http://www.unesco.org/culture/industries/trade/html_eng/question16.shtml, consulted on 29 Sept. 2003

Walras, Léon (1874-1877), *Eléments d'économie pure*

Walras, Léon (1898), *Etudes d'économie politique appliquée*

World Commission on Environment and Development (1987), *Our Common Future*, Oxford & New York, Oxford UP

World Council of Churches (1992), *Christian Faith and the World Economy Today,* a study document

Zwingli, Huldrych (1522), *Eine göttliche Vermahnung an die ältesten Eidgenossen zu Schwyz*

Zwingli, Huldrych (1523) *Von göttlicher und menschlicher Gerechtigkeit*, in *Corpus Reformatorum*, vol 89 (Zwingli Opera vol. II); the page numbers mentioned in the text refer to the *Corpus Reformatorum*

Zwingli, Huldrych (1524), *Eine treue und ernstliche Vermahnung an die frommen Eidgenossen*